An Orange Tree Theatre production

HERE IN AMERICA

by DAVID EDGAR

This play was first performed on
14 September 2024 at the Orange Tree Theatre, Richmond.

ORANGE
TREE
THEATRE
A powerhouse of independent theatre

CAST

Gadg	**Shaun Evans**
Art	**Michael Aloni**
Day	**Faye Castelow**
Miss Bauer	**Jasmine Blackborow**

CREATIVES AND PRODUCTION TEAM

Writer **David Edgar**
Director **James Dacre**
Designer **Simon Kenny**
Lighting Designer **Charles Balfour**
Composer **Valgeir Sigurðsson**
Sound Designer **Bella Kear**
Casting Director **Matilda James CDG**
Voice and Dialect Coach **Aundrea Fudge**
Creative Consultant **Raphael Martin**
Costume Supervisor **Laura Rushton**
Assistant Director **Fiona Munro**
Casting Assistant **Ella Donaldson**
Historical Consultant **Christopher Bigsby**
Wigs supplier and stylist **Elizabeth Marini**
Wigs support **Faye Booth**

Production & Technical Director **Phil Bell**
Production Technician **Priya Virdee**
Company Stage Manager **Jade Gooch**
Deputy Stage Manager **Lizzi Adams**
Deputy Stage Manager **Honor Klein**
Assistant Stage Manager **Nancy O'Melia**
Production Electrician **Chris Galler**
Lead Scenic Artist **Anita Gander**
Scenic Artist **Sophie Firth**

MICHAEL ALONI
Art

This is Michael's UK stage debut.

Theatre credits include *Much Ado About Nothing, An Enemy of the People* (Beer-Sheva Theater); *Ingalea* (Mirror Theater) and *The Idiot* (Studio of Performing Arts).

Television credits include *8200, We Were the Lucky Ones, The Stronghold, The Beauty Queen of Jerusalem, Scenes from a Marriage, Shtisel, Our Boys, Malkot, When Heroes Fly, Temporarily Dead, Hashualim* and *Ha-Shminiya*.

Film credits include *The Stronghold, Love You Charlie, Plan A, Happy Times, Virgins, And Then She Arrived, Antenna, Keep it Cool, A Place in Heaven, Policeman* and *Infiltration*.

JASMINE BLACKBOROW
Miss Bauer

Theatre credits include *Super High Resolution* (Soho Theatre); *The Breach* (Hampstead Theatre); *A Winning Hazard, After October* (Finborough Theatre); *Othello, Much Ado About Nothing* (Pop-up Globe) and *Now This is Not The End* (Arcola Theatre).

Television credits include *The Gentlemen, Marie Antoinette, The Librarians* and *Shadow and Bone*.

Film credits include *Moss and Freud, Odyssey, The Art of Love* and *School's Out Forever*.

FAYE CASTELOW
Day

Orange Tree Theatre credits include: *Audience/Mountain Hotel* and *Leaving*.

Other theatre credits include: *Leopoldstadt* (West End/ Broadway); *Pandemonium* (Soho Theatre/ Wayward Productions); *Man and Superman, After the Dance, Time and the Conways* (National Theatre); *The Witch of Edmonton, The White Devil, The Roaring Girl, The Rover* (RSC); *The Audience* (Nuffield Southampton); *Rattigan's Nijinsky, The Deep Blue Sea* (Chichester Festival Theatre); *The Thrill of Love* (New Vic/St James); *Barefoot in the Park* (Yvonne Arnaud & National Tour); *A Midsummer Night's Dream* (Headlong) and *How To Be An Other Woman* (Gate Theatre).

TV and Film includes: *The Critic, Casualty, Emmerdale, Clique, Pure, Rellik, Father Brown, Inspector George Gently* and *Holby City*.

Radio includes: *Angel Pavement, Rumpole of the Bailey, Pilgrim, The Road to Durham, The Merchant of Venice, Missing Dates* and *Captain Corelli's Mandolin*.

SHAUN EVANS
Gadg

Theatre credits include *Manor* (National Theatre); *Hello/Goodbye* and *Kurt & Syd* (Trafalgar Studios); *Miss Julie* and *Black Comedy*

(Chichester Festival Theatre) and *Blue/Orange* directed by Kathy Burke (Sheffield Crucible).

Shaun is perhaps best known for his portrayal of DS Endeavour Morse in ITV's *Endeavour*. Other TV credits include BBC's *Vigil, The Scandalous Lady W, The Take, The Virgin Queen, Teachers* and the upcoming *Until I Kill You* opposite Anna Maxwell Martin for ITV.

Film credits include *War Book, Being Julia, Gone, Boy* and *Wreckers*.

Directing credits include *Endeavour, Casualty* and *The Bay*.

DAVID EDGAR
Writer

David Edgar has been writing plays professionally since 1971. His original plays for the Royal Shakespeare Company include *Destiny* (1976, John Whiting award), *Maydays* (1983, Plays and Players Best Play award, revived in 2018), *Pentecost* (1994, Evening Standard best play award), *The Prisoner's Dilemma* (2001) and *Written on the Heart* (2011, transferring to the West End in 2012). His new play for the RSC, *The New Real*, opens in October.

His plays for the National Theatre include a new version of his 1985 community play for Dorchester, *Entertaining Strangers* (1988), *The Shape of the Table* (1990), *Albert Speer* (2000) and *Playing with Fire* (2005).

His RSC adaptations include a multi-award-winning adaptation of Dickens' *Nicholas Nickleby* (1980-1, later Channel 4), *Dr Jekyll and Mr Hyde* (1991) and *A Christmas Carol* (2017-2022). In 1978 he wrote an adaptation of *Mary Barnes: Two Accounts of a Journey through Madness* (Birmingham Rep then Royal Court). In 2007 he co-wrote a second play for Dorchester (*A Time to Keep*) with Stephanie Dale; in 2018 he wrote and presented a touring solo show, *Trying it On*. He has written plays for television and extensively for radio, and wrote the 1985 film *Lady Jane*.

David writes regularly for the Guardian, the London Review of Books and other periodicals. He is a past President of the Writers' Guild of Great Britain, which presented him an Outstanding Contribution award in 2023. In 1989 he founded Britain's first graduate playwriting course, at the University of Birmingham, and recently taught on Stephanie Dale's writing course at the Bristol Old Vic Theatre School. His book about playwriting, *How Plays Work*, was published by Nick Hern Books in 2009 and republished in 2021. This year *The Little Black Book of the Populist Right* (written with Jon Bloomfield) was published by Byline Books.

JAMES DACRE
Director

James Dacre is an Olivier and UK Theatre Award-winning Director and Creative Producer who recently launched Living Productions and was Guest Festival Director for Nevill Holt Festival 2024. He was Artistic Director of Royal & Derngate Theatres from 2013-2023 where he produced more than 120 shows, of which 60 toured both nationally and internationally, and 42 transferred to London and were recognised with Olivier, Evening Standard, UK Theatre, WhatsOnStage and The Stage awards. Prior to this, James was Associate Director at the New Vic Theatre, Theatre503 and the National Youth Theatre and directed productions for Shakespeare's Globe, the National Theatre, English Touring Opera, English Touring Theatre, the Royal Exchange Theatre, Theatre Royal Stratford East, The Gate and in the West End and off-Broadway. He is a Board Director of Spirit of 2012, a Trustee for The Theatres Trust and Talawa Theatre Company and a Franco-British Young Leader.

Blue/Orange (Royal & Derngate Northampton); *The Death of a Black Man* (Hampstead); *Footfalls & Rockaby* (Jermyn Street); *The Gift* (Eclipse/Stratford East); *Noughts & Crosses* (Pilot/UK tour); *Red Dust Road* (National Theatre of Scotland); *Rose* (HOME); *Twelfth Night, The Merchant of Venice* (Shakespeare's Globe); *Ghosts* (Theatr Clwyd); *Island* (National Theatre) and BORDER FORCE, an immersive installation/performance/club event for Duckie.

Musical theatre includes *The Lord Of The Rings: A Musical Tale* (Watermill/Chicago Shakespeare Theater/international tour); *Whistle Down The Wind* (Watermill); *The Wiz* (Hope Mill); *Ghost Quartet* (Boulevard Theatre); *Assassins* (Nottingham Playhouse) and the multi award-winning *Sweeney Todd* in a purpose-built pie shop (West End/Off-Broadway).

Other work includes *A Midsummer Night's Dream* and *Le Nozze di Figaro* (Nevill Holt Opera); *Vivienne* (Royal Opera House: Linbury) and *Enthoven Unboxed* (V&A Museum).

SIMON KENNY
Designer

Orange Tree Theatre credits include *Duet For One* (Orange Tree Theatre).

Other theatre credits include *Brassed Off* (Theatre by the Lake); *The Real & Imagined History of The Elephant Man* (Nottingham Playhouse); *Family Tree* (Actors Touring Company);

CHARLES BALFOUR
Lighting Designer

Charles Balfour was born in Stockport but has lived in south London for forty years, so regards himself almost a Southerner.

Theatre credits include *The Corn is Green, Rutherford and Son, Ma Rainey's Black Bottom* (National Theatre); *Romeo and Juliet, A*

Museum in Baghdad, The Seven Acts of Mercy, Miss Littlewood, A Midsummer Night's Dream, The Alchemist, Queen Anne, Hecuba, The Christmas Truce (RSC); Get Up, Stand Up! The Bob Marley Musical, Who's Afraid of Virginia Woolf?, Queen Anne, Richard III, Mojo, Posh, Through the Leaves (West End); The Kite Runner, The River (Broadway); The Prime of Miss Jean Brodie (Donmar Warehouse); The Suppliant Women (Edinburgh Lyceum/Young Vic); Torn, The River, Choir Boy, Chicken Soup with Barley, Now or Later, The Ugly One (Royal Court); The Events (Young Vic/New York Theatre Workshop); The Girlfriend Experience, The Beauty Queen of Leenane (Young Vic); Blue/Orange (Bath Ustinov); Our Lady of Kibeho, The Pope (Northampton); Orlando, The Accrington Pals (Manchester Royal Exchange).

Dance and Opera include Tosca (Karlstad, Sweden); War Requiem, La Triviata (ENO); Sadko, Carmen (Antwerp/Ghent/Bratislava); La Bianca Notte (Hamburg); Carmen, Werther and Saul (Opera North). Over 30 works with the Richard Alston Dance Co. Other choreographers include Wayne McGregor, Aletta Collins and Rosemary Butcher; Scottish, Birmingham, Stuttgart, San Francisco, Atlanta, Vienna Ballets and Beijing Dance Academy.

VALGEIR SIGURÐSSON
Composer

Icelandic composer and producer Valgeir Sigurðsson is known for merging contemporary classical music with electronic innovation. He composes for film, stage, and visual media while maintaining an active presence as a performing musician, with his compositions performed at leading venues and festivals. As the founder and artistic director of Bedroom Community, a label established in 2005 with Nico Muhly and Ben Frost, Valgeir has played a significant role in shaping modern music. His wide-ranging collaborations at Reykjavík's Greenhouse Recording Studios have made him a sought-after producer, engineer, and arranger. He composed We Are in Time, an opera about heart transplants, commissioned by The Scottish Ensemble in 2020. In 2022, he co-created the score for visual artist Sigurður Guðjónsson's Perpetual Motion, showcased at the Icelandic Pavilion during the 59th Venice Biennale. His most recent project Isabelle Lewis is set to release their debut album this year. Valgeir regularly collaborates with director James Dacre, composing scores for productions such as Blue/Orange and Derek Jarman: Modern Nature.

BELLA KEAR
Sound Designer

Bella Kear trained at LAMDA. Her work in theatre includes, as Sound Designer: The Good John Proctor (Offie nominated); Boy in Da Korma and Gustave and

George (Jermyn Street Theatre); *The Great Murder Mystery* (The Lost Estate) ; *Invisible* (Bush Theatre and New York); *Elephant and Clutch* (Bush Studio); *The Night Woman* (The Other Palace); *The Animal Kingdom* (Hampstead Theatre); *Outpatient* and *Oh Calm Down* (Summerhall Fringe 2024).

As Associate or Assistant Sound Designer: *Mnemonic (*National Theatre); *Newsies (*Troubadour Theatre); *Liberation Squares* (Nottingham Playhouse); *Silence* (Donmar Warehouse); *Edith* at (The Lowry); *Blue/Orange* (Theatre Royal Bath and tour); *Seven Methods of Killing Kylie Jenner (*Riksteatern); *A Place for We* (Park Theatre) and *Sizwe Banzi is Dead* (MAST Mayflower Studios and tour).

Other projects include *Mudlarking*, a sound installation at the Bush Theatre.

MATILDA JAMES CDG
Casting Director

Originally from Cornwall, Matilda works in casting for theatre, screen, and games. As Casting Director at Shakespeare's Globe from 2012-2017, she cast over 50 shows for the Globe and Sam Wanamaker Playhouse.

A founding member of The Murmuration, a women-led theatre and arts producing collective, her recent collaborations include work with the Barbican; York Theatre Royal and Kyiv City Ballet; #Merky Films; and Citizens of the World, the UK's leading choir for people seeking sanctuary and asylum.

Orange Tree Theatre casting credits include *Red Speedo, Suite in Three Keys, Testmatch* and *Uncle Vanya*.

Other recent casting for theatre includes: *The House Party* (Chichester Festival Theatre / Headlong); *A Child of Science* (Bristol Old Vic); *QUIZ* (Wessex Grove / JCTP); *2.22 A Ghost Story (*West End and on tour); *Family Tree* (Actors Touring Company / Belgrade Theatre Coventry / Brixton House) and *Gin Craze!* (Northampton Royal & Derngate / English Touring Theatre).

Film includes: *Portraits of Dangerous Women, Benjamin* and *Pond Life*.

AUNDREA FUDGE
Voice and Dialect Coach

Aundrea Fudge is an accent/dialect and speech coach from New York. She completed her MFA in Voice Studies from the Royal Central School of Speech and Drama in 2018 and is currently based in London.

Orange Tree Theatre credits include *Red Speedo, Meetings* and *Yellowman*.

Theatre includes *Slave Play* (Noël Coward Theatre); *Skeleton Crew, Clyde's* (Donmar Warehouse); *Choir Boy* (Bristol Old Vic); *The House Party* (Chichester); *A Raisin in the Sun, A View From The Bridge* (UK Tour/ Headlong); *Start Swimming!* (Young Vic); *The Enormous Crocodile, Once on this Island* (Regents Park

Open Air); *Between Riverside and Crazy, Blackout Songs* (Hampstead); *Bootycandy* (Gate Theatre); *Refilwe* (Bernie Grant Arts Centre); *Cinderella* (Brixton House); *Driving Miss Daisy* (Barn Theatre) and *Bring it on! The Musical* (Southbank Centre). Film includes *Bernard & The Genie, Locked In-Film* and *Wheel of Time*.

TV includes *Andor* (Season 2).

RAPHAEL MARTIN
Creative Consultant

Raphael Martin is the Director of The Lit Shop Ltd, a theatrical literary management company which acts as dramaturg, literary manager, and creative producer for theatre companies and institutions on a consulting basis.

Current and previous clients include: Theatr Clwyd; Oxford Stage; Belgrade Coventry; National Youth Theatre; Rose Theatre Kingston; National Theatre School of Canada; English Touring Theatre; Northampton Royal & Derngate; Gate Theatre Dublin; Second Half Productions; Royal Shakespeare Company; Chichester Festival Theatre; Seattle Rep; Malthouse Theatre Melbourne; Madison Wells Live (Broadway); National Theatre of Wales; Royal Welsh College of Music and Drama; Elliott Harper Productions; Peaky Blinders: The Rise (Hartshorn-Hook/Immersive Everywhere); Harrow School, and Living Productions.

Previous to The Lit Shop Ltd he worked at the following institutions: Manhattan Theatre Club; Soho Rep; Sonia Friedman Productions; The Gate Notting Hill; the Bush Theatre; the Royal Court Young Writers Programme; the National Theatre, and The Susan Smith Blackburn Award.

LAURA RUSHTON
Costume Supervisor

Laura trained at London College of Fashion.

Theatre credits include: *Shifters* (Duke of York's Theatre); *Burlesque The Musical* (UK tour); *Starter For Ten* (Bristol Old Vic); *La Cage Aux Folles* (Regents Park Open Air Theatre); *The Spy Who Came In From The Cold, Local Hero* and *Never Have I Ever* (Chichester Festival Theatre); *Quiz* (Tour); *Macbeth, The Captive Queen, The White Devil, Knight Of The Burning Pestle* And *Thomas Tallis* (Sam Wanamaker Playhouse); *I, Joan, Eyam, King Lear, Macbeth* and *The Oresteia* (Shakespeare's Globe); *Taming Of The Shrew* and *Henry Rebellion/ War Of The Roses* (RSC); *A Christmas Carol* and *Peter Pan* (Rose Theatre).

Opera credits include: *Magic Flute* (Welsh National Opera); *Silent Night* (Opera North); *Cosi Fan Tutte* (Northern Ireland Opera); *Don Giovanni* and *Barber Of Seville* (Nevill Holt Opera Festival).

Dance credits include: *Show* (Hofesh Shechter Company);

Deadclub (Fuel); *Mothers* (The Place) and *The Roof* (Fuel).

FIONA MUNRO
Assistant Director

Fiona is currently training on the MFA in Theatre Directing at Birkbeck.

As Director: *Faustine* (The Hope Theatre/The Quarry/The Cockpit); *The Merchant of Venice* (The Golden Goose); *Saving Jonah* (The Cockpit) and *Much Ado About Nothing* (Pendley Manor).

As Assistant Director: *An All American Funeral* (RCSSD); *A Midsummer Night's Dream* (The Attic Theatre); *Malpractice* (The Bread and Roses); *Rally for the Rose* (The Rose Playhouse); *Twelfth Night* (CSVPA) and *Pericles* (The Mumford Theatre).

CHRISTOPHER BIGSBY
Historical Consultant

An emeritus professor in American Studies at the University of East Anglia, Christopher Bigsby is an award-winning academic, novelist, and biographer.

A Fellow of the Royal Society of Literature and the Royal Society of Arts, he has published more than sixty books. He is especially known for his work on the American theatre, including a two-volume biography of Arthur Miller together with a critical account of his work as playwright, novelist, short story writer and essayist. Recently, he

has published three volumes on American playwrights who began their careers in this century, the most recent being *American Dramatists in the 21st Century*. Together with Malcolm Bradbury he has written plays for radio and television and for many years was a presenter on BBC Radio 4. His latest novel is *Dreamcatcher*. He is also author of a volume of poems, *In the Face of Darkness*.

LIZZI ADAMS
Deputy Stage Manager

Theatre credits include *People, Places & Things* (Trafalgar Theatre); *Jekyll & Hyde* (National Theatre Schools tour); *I, Daniel Blake* (UK tour); *The Winston Machine* (UK tour); *A Christmas Carol* (Shakespeare North Playhouse); *A Midsummers Night Dream* (Shakespeare North Playhouse and Northern Stage); *The Blue Man Group* (world tour); *Marys Seacole* (Donmar Warehouse); *The Keyworkers Cycle* (Almeida Theatre); *Wendy & Peter Pan* (Leeds Playhouse); *Oliver Twist* (UK tour and NT at Home); *Beryl, Seagulls, Treasure Island* and *The Rise and Fall of Little Voice* (Octagon Theatre, Bolton); *Aladdin* (The Floral Pavilion, New Brighton); *Nina: A Story of Me and Nina Simone* (UK and Ireland tour); *Shirleymander* (The Playground Theatre, London); *The Toyboy Diaries* and *Parade* (Hope Mill Theatre, Manchester); *Hair*: 50th Anniversary Performance (The Vaults); *Women Beware Women* (Camden's People Theatre) and various others.

HONOR KLEIN
Deputy Stage Manager

Honor Klein trained at the Royal
Welsh College of Music and
Drama, graduating in 2019
she has since worked as a
freelance stage manager in and
around London.

Theatre Credits include: *The End*
(Bush Theatre); *The Watsons*
(Mountview); *The Bleeding Tree*
(Southwark Playhouse); *Breeding*
(King's Head Theatre); *The Good
John Proctor* (Jermyn Street
Theatre); *Cinderella* and *The
Coronation of Poppea* (English
Touring Opera); *As We Face The
Sun* (Bush Theatre); *Barnum's
Bird* (Royal College of Music);
2:22 A Ghost Story (Criterion
Theatre); *Ava: The Secret
Conversations* (Riverside Studios);
The Magic Flute (Royal College of
Music); *Curious* (Soho Theatre);
The Tide (Talawa); 2021 & 2020
Summer Theatre Festival (Roman
Theatre); *Peter Pan* (Alban Arena)
and *Triple Bill* (Royal College
of Music).

NANCY O'MELIA
Assistant Stage Manager

Nancy Is a freelance Assistant
Stage Manager based in London.
She completed her drama school
training in Theatre Production
Arts (Stage Management) at
Mountview Academy of Theatre
Arts in 2022.

Theatre Credits include: ASM/
Book Cover *Paranormal Activity*
(Leeds Playhouse); ASM/Book
Cover *Mamma Mia* UK and
International Tour and Dep ASM
Deathdrop (Criterion Theatre).

ORANGE TREE THEATRE
A powerhouse of independent theatre

We are a local theatre with a global reputation.

A show at the Orange Tree is close-up magic: live, entertaining, unmissable. We're an intimate theatre with the audience wrapped around the stage. We believe in celebrating what it means to be human. We believe in putting people at the centre of the stories we tell. And we believe in the power of a writer's words, an actor's voice, and an audience's imagination to transport us to other worlds and other lives.

We punch above our weight to create world-class productions of new and contemporary drama, revitalise classics and re-discoveries, and introduce children and young people to the magic of theatre.

We are deeply rooted in our local community in South West London. We work with thousands of people aged 0 to 100 in Richmond and beyond through participatory theatre, bringing generations together to build confidence, connection, and joy. Our ground-breaking Primary Shakespeare and Shakespeare Up Close projects pack the theatre with children and ignite a spark to last a lifetime.

We're a registered charity (266128). With only 180 seats and no support from Arts Council England, we rely on the generosity of our audiences and donors to raise £650,000 a year. These funds support our outstanding work on stage and in the community and invest in the next generation of talent.

Artistic Director **Tom Littler**
Executive Director **Hanna Streeter**

orangetreetheatre.co.uk

LONDON BOROUGH OF
RICHMOND UPON THAMES

OT TEAM

Executive
Executive Director and Joint CEO
Hanna Streeter
Artistic Director and Joint CEO
Tom Littler
Executive Assistant Reya Muller

Producing and Programming
General Manager & Producer
Sarah Murray
Literary Associate William Gregory
Carne Associate Director
Natasha Rickman**
Casting Associate Matilda James
CDG*
Resident Assistant Director
(Birkbeck) Rosie Tricks
Trainee Production Assistant
Hetty Opayinka

Production and Technical
Production & Technical Director
Phil Bell
Company Stage Manager
Jade Gooch
Production Technician Priya Virdee

Community
Community Director Francesca Ellis
Community Officer Madi Mahoney
Community Associate
Jess Haygarth*
Community Facilitators
Jordana Golbourn, Ed Hill,
Amy Tickner
Community Assistants
Sophie Kenyon, Mais Robinson

Development
Development Director
Dominique Trotter
Development Officer Katie Devey
Memberships & Sales Coordinator
Rosa Stilitz

*Denotes Freelance or Agency
**The Carne Associate Director
position is generously supported
by Philip and Christine Carne

Marketing
Marketing & Sales Director
(maternity leave) Rachel Wood
Marketing & Sales Director
(maternity cover) Meg Eyre
Marketing Officer Hannah McLelland
Box Office & Sales Coordinator
Addie Uglow
Graphic Designer Annie Rushton*
PR Kate Morley PR*

Finance, HR and operations
Deputy Executive Director
Julie Weston
Finance Manager Caroline Goodwin
Finance Associate Jodie
Cramphorn*
HR Consultants Bendy Ashfield and
Greg Jauncey for Theatre People*

Customer Service
Front of House Manager
Ben Purkiss
Duty Managers Leonie Crawford,
Andrew Davidson, Tyler Deniro,
Jay Hannaford, Fenella Machin
Stewards Ailsa Auchnie, Eden Igwe,
Georgina Barley, Irie Page, Juliet
Mills, Kaitlin Reynell, Kevin Mandry,
Lucy Greenhalgh, Luiza McDowell,
Madeleine Paine, Maire McGovern,
Marie Diby, Martha Barnett, Penny
Cranford, Shane Convery, Sophie
Kenyon, Tomas Caldon, Daisy
Shaw, Martin Alfonsin Larsen,
Roanna Mcivor
*Cleaner (from Miss Merry Cleaning
Services)* Viktor Kirov

Board Members
Feras Al-Chalabi, Anita Arora,
Carolyn Backhouse, Richard
Buxton, Judy Gibbons *(Chair)*,
Lesley Gregory, Marina Jones,
Victoria Kent, Robert Lisney, David
Marks, Corinne Meredith, India
Semper-Hughes, Harriet Varley
Chair Emeritus Richard Humphreys

HERE IN AMERICA

David Edgar

To Jonathan Church

Characters

GADG
ART
DAY
MISS BAUER

Setting

Mainly in Connecticut in late March 1952.

Also in New York in 1962–3.

Notation

A forward slash (/) indicates when the next speaker begins speaking.

This text went to press before the end of rehearsals and so may differ slightly from the play as performed.

Scene One

Central Park in New York. A fine day in late 1962. GADG *is fifty-three,* ART *is forty-six.* GADG *holds a script.*

ART. So, did you read it?

GADG. How ya doin', toots?

ART. Hi, Gadg, thanks for coming. Did you read it?

GADG. Why are we in Central Park?

ART. It's a lovely day. So –

GADG. We could stroll over to the Tavern on the Green. Do lunch.

ART. Or we could talk right here.

GADG. Where we won't be seen together.

ART. I… I didn't say that.

GADG. No.

Slight pause.

ART. So did you read it?

GADG. Sure.

ART. And?

GADG. Well, it's easy to spot what it's about. Who it's about.

ART. Which is why I'm asking you to do it.

GADG. Cos you could say, I'm the last guy in the world…

ART. I said it, Gadg. You're the best director in America. Why wouldn't I want you to direct my play?

GADG. Being a character, as you might say.

ART. Well, in a manner of / speaking...

GADG. And thereby, in the very best of company.

Pause.

ART. What do you mean?

GADG. So did you make her funeral? The other character? Our 'Her'?

ART. No.

GADG. Why not?

ART. I figured that she'd not be there.

Slight pause.

Sometimes I forget she was ours. That we have her in common.

Slight pause.

I still have her bicycle.

GADG. Her in common too.

ART. What do you mean?

GADG. As my wife is wont to remark: 'There's these two Joes. And they share a story so remarkably similar they could be brothers. Or even, the same guy. So how the fuck is it, they don't speak for ten years?

ART. Well, Molly of all people knows / that –

GADG. How did that happen? How'd you tell that story?

ART. I have told that story, Gadg. It's the story of the play.

Slight pause.

So did she like it? Molly?

GADG, *so-so gesture.*

GADG. She had trouble with the flashbacks.

ART. Like she did with *Salesman.*

GADG. Sure.

ART. Except of course that in *Salesman* they weren't
flashbacks. She said they were flashbacks, which is why she
tried to have you strip them out.

GADG. Which of course I / didn't –

ART. They were memories, that popped into his mind. Not
always accurately. Well, almost never accurately. Like our
memories.

GADG. Which is exactly how / I directed –

ART. Which pop up in our minds, when we're saying other
things.

GADG. What, like they're doing now?

ART. Yeah. Like they're doing now. Like I learnt at college.
How the art of theatre is the hidden past and how it shudders
back to life.

GADG. And threatens everything.

Slight pause.

ART. So will you do it?

GADG. Will you let me do it how I want? Say what I like?

ART. As long as I can too.

GADG. I'll let you know. Tomorrow. Over lunch. In a fucking
restaurant.

Scene Two

*Ten years earlier. The living room of the Kazans' house in Sandy
Hook, Connecticut, spring 1952. There's a drinks cabinet.* DAY
*is forty-five, tall and elegant, in slacks. She is inspecting a
Scrabble board set out on a coffee table. A dictionary is nearby.
A grandfather clock strikes eleven.*

DAY. Info?

> *She checks a dictionary and then calls.*

> 'Info'?

> *Enter* GADG, *towelling his head. He is forty-two.*

GADG. So what's the problem?

DAY. Since when is 'info' a word?

GADG. When I ask for it.

DAY. You ask for 'info'?

GADG. All the time. I've covered up the deck.

> *He drops the towel on a chair.* DAY *shows him the open dictionary.*

DAY. Obsequious surrender, please.

GADG. Who introduced this instrument of torture to our house?

DAY. My mother.

GADG. So no surprise I'm stuck.

> DAY *turns his rack round.*

DAY. You can have 'info'.

GADG. Thanks.

DAY. And in fact you've got an M. And a blank tile which could be an R.

> *She turns 'INFO' into 'INFORM'.*

> And, lo, you have one two six seven nothing ten points for your pains. Whilst I – annoyingly…

> *She puts a Y before the O.*

> …have a mere eight plus one is nine.

GADG. 'Yo'?

> DAY *opens the dictionary at a marked place.*

DAY. 'Interjection calling for attention.'

GADG. Well, no shit.

DAY. Is it still raining?

GADG. Yup.

DAY. He's driving from New York?

GADG. Sure is.

DAY (*picking up* GADG*'s towel and folding it*). And did he deign to vouchsafe when he'd actually appear?

GADG (*looks at his watch*). An hour ago.

DAY. And what d'you think he wants?

GADG. It's what I want, I asked him.

DAY. I know that. But he said he'd make the trip. He wants something.

GADG. He's headed north. Connecticut is on the way.

DAY. That doesn't actually answer my / question –

GADG. Maybe he wants to find out what I want.

DAY. As he will.

GADG. Or maybe he just wants to offer me a play.

DAY. He'd mail it you.

GADG. Not if he's dropping by.

DAY. How's things with him and Mary?

GADG, *so-so gesture*.

Is there still someone else?

GADG. Still?

DAY. The mystery woman in Los Angeles.

GADG. Oh, yeah, well.

DAY. Oh yeah well what?

GADG. I told you. There was a starlet at a party.

DAY. And you were at this party?

GADG. Sure. But it was for Arthur Miller.

DAY. So it ain't just meetings after all.

GADG. No, funnily / enough –

DAY. And the writer gets first pick of the talent?

GADG. No...

DAY. And did she have a name? Miss Oh Yeah Well?

GADG (*pleased*). Miss Bauer.

DAY. First name?

GADG. Didn't need one. Next day, we take her to a meeting – meeting – as our secretary. So I say 'Did you get that down, Miss Bauer?' and she says, 'Yes, of course, Mr Kazan.'

DAY. But Bauer ain't her name.

GADG. No, not remotely.

DAY. What a hoot. And the occasion for this merry prank?

GADG. When we tried to sell the shorefront film to Columbia.

DAY. That's before or after Art pulled out?

GADG. When he refused to change the script to turn the racketeers from mobsters into communists. And lost the movie.

DAY. And did the delectable Miss Bauer note that down?

GADG. Look. She's a sweet girl. Had a hard time as a kid. Worked in an airplane factory in the war, and then bit parts in movies. He bought her some poems and copies of his plays. God knows what she made of them. I think he may have signed a photograph. He kissed her at the airport.

DAY. Oh, yeah?

We hear the arrival of a car from outside.

GADG. As he left.

DAY. So, cute.

Car door opens and bangs shut, children's voices.

GADG. Is that him?

DAY. The kids. Will he want lunch?

GADG. We don't know what he wants.

DAY. Fix him a cocktail.

GADG (*glances at his watch*). Day, Art's a puritan.

DAY. So does she know?

GADG. Does who know what?

DAY. Mary. About the sweetly surreptitious 'Miss Bauer'.

GADG. Hey, you know what? I don't think Art told her.

DAY. And did you sign a photograph?

GADG. Why would / I –

DAY. You said Art signed the doll a photograph.

GADG (*'as if'*). Honey, that was him, and this is me.

Slight pause.

DAY. Right. Chalk and cheese.

GADG. You don't agree?

DAY. You two.

GADG *looks questioningly at* DAY. *She goes to* GADG *and touches his shoulder.*

What the whole world knows.

GADG. I don't.

DAY. With maybe two exceptions.

GADG. So?

DAY. Two men who could be brothers. One Greek, one a Jew. Both sons of fathers who come here from someplace far away, and set up businesses, and lose them in the greatest crash in history. And they work their way through college, one by waiting tables and the other writing plays. And they decide the crash was all the fault of the wicked capitalist

system which needed overthrowing Tuesday at the very
latest. But who nonetheless both end back in New York City
basking in Fame, Fortune and Success. Oh, and both married
to two good ol' straight-backed Yankee girls.

And the only real difference is that one of them is a member
of the Group – allegedly the most important theatre company
on earth – where they call him Gadget, because whether it's
a sticky scene change or the meaning of Act Two, he's the
one they call upon to fix it.

GADG. I see. So who exactly are these people?

She lightly punches his shoulder.

One, married very happily.

DAY. Really?

GADG. Really.

DAY. I am glad to hear that.

GADG. And of course, the good ol' girls weren't so sold on
capitalism either.

DAY. But of course there were differences as well as
similarities.

GADG. Like what?

DAY. Well, only one was going to make it in the movies. And
win a best director Oscar for *Gentleman's Agreement*.

GADG. Sure, but Art did write / *Death of* –

DAY. But not for *A Streetcar Named Desire*.

Pause. GADG *says nothing.*

DAY. Which is why, when you say what you're going to say,
you're not seeking his permission. You're not asking him,
you're telling him.

GADG. Of course.

DAY *picking up the folded towel to take out.*

DAY. Good. I'm going to fix the kids some lunch while you fix
me a cocktail.

GADG. Right.

He stands. Something has caught DAY*'s eye, outside.*

DAY. Hear this. Do you want to know how it begins?

GADG. How what begins?

DAY. The movie of today.

GADG. No, how?

DAY (*still looking through the window*). Exterior, house, morning. A man sits in his car. Finishes his cigarette, alights. Walks to the house, and enters.

GADG *looks at her. She goes out.*

Scene Three

A few moments later. GADG, *and* DAY *in a cooking apron.* ART *is there. He's thirty-six. Everyone holds cocktails.*

ART. Old fashioned?

GADG. Yeah.

ART. It's a 1951 Studebaker convertible. I regard it as the best car in the world.

DAY. The cocktail.

ART. Oh.

GADG. Day's favourite.

DAY. Our favourite.

ART. Well, cheerio.

ART *takes a sip.*

Sweet.

GADG. Sugar.

ART. And yet strangely bitter.

DAY. That'd be the bitters.

ART. Bourbon?

DAY. Rye. Artie Miller, welcome to our lovely home.

She and ART *embrace.*

ART. Molly.

DAY. Call me Day.

ART (*the drink*). Thanks.

DAY. How're the kids?

ART. Terrific. Robert's a great pitcher and in the fall he starts off at the Little Red.

DAY. The little what?

GADG. It's a school in Greenwich Village. All the kids go there.

DAY. Do they.

ART. And yours?

DAY. Great pitching also. Mary?

ART. Fine and dandy.

GADG. Art. Sit down.

ART goes to the coffee table and sees the Scrabble.

ART (*the Scrabble*). What's this?

DAY. Oh, it's the new intelligent time-killer. Quite the rage.

GADG. Given us by Mother Day.

ART sits and looks at the board.

ART. It's a kind of – crossword?

DAY. Kind of.

ART. Why the numbers on the letters?

DAY sits.

DAY. It's the score. From one to ten.

ART. Depending on?

DAY. Its frequency of use in the English language. So D and G are two, F four and X is eight.

GADG. And in the Polish version, zee is one.

ART. There's a Polish version?

GADG. No, it's just / a joke –

ART (*picking up one of* DAY*'s tiles*). So here's a zee.

GADG. Uh, strictly speaking –

DAY. So I'd left an open I and Gadg had N, F and O and claimed that 'info' was a word, which I accepted for a quiet life but also it's the first time that he's played it and it gave him 'Info' but he also had an M and a blank tile which I deemed to be an R.

ART. And you can do that?

DAY. Surely can. Which left me an open O before which I could pop my Y.

ART. 'Yo'?

GADG. They must be real words.

ART. Then I repeat the question.

DAY. Five points but because it's on a / double –

GADG. Daughter Day insists that Yo's / a word –

DAY. The dictionary insists that / it's –

ART. 'Zho.'

He removes the Y from 'YO', takes a Z and H from DAY*'s rack and puts the letters in front of the O.*

DAY. I beg your pardon?

GADG. 'Zho'?

ART. Zee, H, O. It's a kind of cow.

GADG. I repeat the 'Zho'?

ART. From the Himalayas.

GADG. How in the name of all that's / holy –

DAY. Look it up.

    GADG *quickly sits down and looks it up.*

ART. So that is – fifteen points. What does 'double word' mean?

DAY. You get thirty. If it's a / word.

GADG (*dictionary*). Fuck you, Miller.

DAY (*to cover the profanity*). So, Artie, are you writing?

    The three sit with their cocktails.

ART. I'm nearly writing. Well, I think I am.

DAY. How can you only think you're nearly doing something?

ART. I mean, I haven't yet decided if I want to write it.

DAY. Do you have – one of those things that playwrights have?

ART. A typewriter?

DAY. A theme.

ART. I have a theme.

DAY. Is it the usual?

ART. The usual?

DAY. Gadg ran into Cliff Odets the other day.

ART. Oh, yes?

DAY. He was back from Hollywood to bask in the *Golden Boy* revival. And he told / Gadg that –

GADG. And show off his new Cadillac.

ART (*to* GADG). And he told Gadg what?

DAY (*throwing a glance at* GADG). Oh, he said you'd done the manifest iniquity of American capitalism, the obvious impossibility of the American Dream, and the clear moral inadequacy of the American Marriage, and maybe now you should get off the fence.

DAY *stands*.

Of course, the big problem with Odets isn't just that he thinks that he's as good as Chekhov – which is just an everyday regular two-bit playwriterly delusion – but that he goes and tells that to the newspapers. Promise me you won't do that.

ART. Promise. Something smells good.

DAY. So do you want some lunch?

GADG. What is it?

DAY. Corned beef hash.

GADG *a glance at* ART, *who gives a look of unconvincing enthusiasm*.

GADG. Cheese and crackers?

ART. Sure.

DAY. Missing a treat.

She goes out.

ART. So how ya doin', toots?

GADG. I'm swell. Hey, thanks for coming.

ART. It's on my way.

GADG. So, where / are you –

ART. So what's Day's beef with Cliff Odets?

GADG. Day never really liked the Group Theatre.

ART. I thought she was a critic for *New Theatre* magazine. Didn't all those guys / adore –

GADG. And her great-grandfather was President of Yale.

Slight pause.

ART. Well, I thought *Awake and Sing* was a work of genius.

GADG. Ah, but you didn't see *Waiting for Lefty*.

ART. Wish I had. Your finest hour?

GADG. Sure was.

ART. And that's the one when you're planted in the audience...

GADG. And then, at a crucial / moment...

ART. – moment –

GADG. I leap on stage to expose the dirty rat who was plotting to betray the heroic proletariat.

ART. With some deathless line no doubt.

GADG. I may have mentioned that the Son of Cain was by coincidence my lousy brother.

ART *laughs*.

So kind of a surprise that it remains the best night of my life.

ART. Still?

GADG. Yes, still.

ART. Gadg, I'm so sorry about *Streetcar* at the Oscars.

Slight pause.

GADG. Ah, yuh. Well.

ART. Do you think it was the League of Decency?

GADG. No, I don't. In fact, I know it wasn't.

Slight pause.

I had lunch with Darryl Zanuck. Head of Fox. And he explained exactly why I didn't get the Oscar.

Slight pause.

ART. The darkness of the day.

GADG. Cliff is frightened for his movie.

ART. What, that they might not release it?

GADG. So he fears. And so Zanuck said –

ART. You know the League 'pointed out' to Columbia that I'd failed to take out an ad condemning communism. That's not 'supporting' it. But failing to condemn it. Prove a negative.

GADG. Yeah. Well, that's always / tough –

ART. And they're banning school books which refer to poverty or segregation. Or hot-lunch programmes.

GADG. Really?

ART. On the grounds that those are clearly communist positions. And the FBI are insisting librarians tell them what books people borrow.

GADG. Kidding.

ART. And faculty at the University of California have to take an oath of loyalty or be fired.

GADG. You don't say.

ART. As they do say, 'Don't collect your thoughts, you'll be indicted for unlawful assembly.'

GADG *laughs. Enter* DAY *with a well-laid-out tray of cheese, crackers and fruit. The laughter stops.*

Not that it's funny.

GADG. No.

DAY (*putting the plate down on the table*). So what's not funny?

ART. In fact, I've been asked to sign a petition...

DAY. Upon what topic?

GADG. Teachers and librarians.

DAY. Is this more fans?

ART. No, a petition.

DAY (*slight shrug*). So you said.

ART. And don't you ask yourself, why this is happening? Now?

DAY. And what d'you / think –

ART. Well, I'd say it's because of 'Losing China'. As if we owned it in the first place. The need to shore up our imperial pretensions. Oh, and getting the Democrats out of the White House for all time?

Pause. He cuts a piece of cheese.

Thanks.

DAY. And China's / such –

ART (*the knife handle*). Say, are these your initials?

GADG. Wedding present.

DAY. Not a wedding present. And China's such a great thing?

ART. What, the masses overthrowing their oppressors? Hell, yeah.

DAY. You don't think, that's a tad / simplistic?

ART. And of course what's going on out west.

DAY. What's that?

ART. What, apart from the Hollywood Ten? Then the Hollywood Nineteen and now the Hollywood Pretty Much Everybody?

DAY. I think that's maybe a *slight* / exaggeration –

ART. And not to mention Larry Parks and all the others naming names. And, for chrissakes, Gadg's Oscar.

Pause.

GADG. No big deal.

ART. Oh, yeah? So by what criterion is *American in Paris* a better picture than *Streetcar Named Desire*? Apart from the affiliations and beliefs of the director?

DAY. Well –

GADG. Well, we're agreed on that.

ART. I hope we're agreed on pretty much everything.

A tricky pause. ART *looks at the Scrabble board and finds a joke.*

'Info', 'Inform'. If you had an E and R you'd be really topical.

DAY (*'Are you going to tell him now?'*). Gadg?

ART (*'Why is she asking that?'*). 'Gadg'?

GADG. Day has this theory. That we're basically the same person.

DAY. Day also has this theory that you ought / to tell –

ART. What, like...

GADG. Immigrant fathers. Losing everything in the Depression.

ART. True enough.

GADG. Working through college.

ART. Turning left.

DAY. Speaking of which –

GADG. Making it in the entertainment business.

ART. That too.

DAY. And –

GADG. But maybe... differences as well as similarities.

ART. Well, your pop sold carpeting and mine sold coats.

GADG. And I'm a Greek and you're a Jew.

ART. So, there's that theory down the pan.

DAY. But nonetheless, / they both –

ART. So what's all this about?

Pause.

You said that we had something to discuss. Are we discussing it?

Pause.

GADG. Just a catch-up. It's been a while.

ART. Gadg, it didn't sound like it was just a catch-up, on the phone.

DAY. Did you say, it had / stopped raining?

ART *stands*.

ART. You see, my theory is that they want to kill off the New Deal. The Roosevelt legacy. Which showed how if the country's in a hole, you don't keep digging, you take action, you get people back to work, you build roads and dams and bridges and even make a picture or produce a play or two. And if they can persuade America all that was just a plot to hand the country over to a foreign power, then we can dump the whole shebang and get back to what our fathers held to be the normal way of things. Here in America. And the places where we felt safe – where we had the right to feel safe – aren't safe any more. I mean, for Christ's sake, Gadg. Isn't that how it looks to you?

GADG. Well, that's an argument.

ART. An *argument*? So didn't you write a play about Dimitroff?

GADG. Yeah, with Art Smith.

DAY. Dimitroff.

ART (*to* DAY). He was the guy who the Nazis put on trial for / burning down –

DAY. Burning down the Reichstag. Strangely, I knew that.

ART. And who unlike the studio heads, including Darryl Zanuck, stood up to them. On the grounds that he was innocent. Kind of a useful lesson from the past, that might apply to what's happening today.

DAY. Did you say, it had stopped raining?

GADG. Yeah.

DAY. So why don't you boys take a walk. Gadg can show you where the pipes are leaking.

GADG. They're not leaking.

DAY. Gadg can show you where the pipes aren't leaking.

GADG. Hard to tell, today.

ART. I mean, unless you see that as 'simplistic'.

DAY *goes and picks up the remains of the crackers*.

DAY. Well, Art. You always make great speeches. I'll go see to the kids.

(*As she goes*.) The napkins are monogrammed as well.

DAY *leaves with the plates, passing* MISS BAUER, *entering. Perhaps she is on a bicycle. She is twenty-six years old. She wears shorts and a sweater, and has Harlow-blonde hair.*

MISS BAUER. So here I am.

ART (*to* GADG). So did you see her?

GADG. Who? Where?

MISS BAUER. And see, it's spring.

ART (*to* GADG). Hollywood, and you know who.

MISS BAUER (*to* GADG). When you first found me, crying on an empty sound stage. And introduced me to Art.

GADG. 'Mr Arthur Miller, the distinguished playwright.'

MISS BAUER. Why, I'm so shamed.

ART. You shouldn't be.

MISS BAUER. And the next day, you invite me to join you taking an important meeting at Columbia...

GADG (*to* MISS BAUER) 'Miss Bauer, take a letter.'

MISS BAUER. And a party, where I'm on the list as 'Kazan Girl'.

ART. And to a bookstore.

MISS BAUER. Where you give me the *Poems of Walt Whitman* and a copy of your play. Which rests on my bedside table now.

ART. And every man who lays his eyes on her...

GADG. Including you…

MISS BAUER. And there's a poor man slumped against the outer door, look, with his dog. Don't move them!

ART. I'll give him a dollar.

MISS BAUER (*to* GADG). And you tell me I should go work with the Actor's Lab. A girl like me! And I'm told by people called things like Bromberg and Carnovsky about the Group Theatre in New York, with 'improv' and exercises. Take three words and make a play. 'Bread, people, pain.' And how different it all is from how they do things here in Hollywood, where it's all angles and your eyeline and the light.

GADG. 'Pages, weather…'

MISS BAUER. 'Waiting.'

GADG. Waiting.

MISS BAUER. And I confess I've never seen a play. And now to read these plays from the time when I was being shunted round from foster home to foster home. And how some people made a killing from the war but the poor just go on getting poorer.

ART. And I give her my signed picture, at the airport. And I fly back east, with her perfume on my hands. And I think, 'when…'

GADG. 'Studebaker. Freeway.

MISS BAUER. And it being – just – that simple.

GADG. 'Girl.'

MISS BAUER (*to* GADG). And one day you tell me that the face I'm seeing's not your real face. And I ask why. And you tell me the story of a Greek god who put on a mask so people couldn't see his real feelings. But years later he tired of it and tried to take it off. But it wouldn't come. 'Face. Gadget. Mask.'

GADG. And both marry stern and brittle women of unbending moral disposition. And both look elsewhere.

They both look at MISS BAUER.

ART. Ain't that just…

Re-enter DAY. *She's taken off her apron.*

DAY. So, you boys still here?

GADG. Just going.

DAY. And the conversation?

Slight pause.

GADG. This and that.

ART. Shooting the breeze.

DAY (*to* GADG). You're telling him.

She goes out. ART *looks questioningly at* GADG. GADG *gestures that* ART *follow him, and goes out.* ART *turns to* MISS BAUER.

ART. So tell me what they tell you at the Lab.

The scene changes as MISS BAUER *speaks to* ART.

MISS BAUER. So this is how it works. It's from the Russian theatre, and it's called 'affective memory'. Your character feels a strong emotion in the play, and the actor wants to make that true and real. So you think about something similar which happened in your past. But not just to remember it, but to relive it, how it was. Where it happened, what you were wearing, what the other people wore. The sounds, the smells, the touches. And when you've got that, and you've felt what you were feeling then, you can bring it back, each time you play the scene.

It's called 'the magic if'. What you'd do if it was you.

So your character is lost and you remember the first night in the home that wasn't your home because you didn't have one. Or she's in pain and you smell the way a rabbit smells when someone makes you skin it and then cook it. The varnish on an airplane fuselage. The kind of cough the dog made when she died. Or the breath upon your neck when you don't want the breath upon your neck.

And just sometimes how it feels to have someone's arms around you and you want them to be there.

And the way Elia does it is, he comes up to you and leans into you and whispers. Rabbit. Varnish. Breath.

She goes out. ART *turns to see* GADG, *standing in the wood.*

Scene Four

The woods behind GADG *and* DAY*'s house. There's a fallen log, maybe a rock or a tree stump.* GADG *holds a football he's found.* ART *turns to him.*

GADG. You first?

ART. You invited me.

GADG. You came.

ART *smiles.* GADG *throws him the football.*

ART. Alright. It's after *All My Sons*. I decide to go and do some real work.

GADG. Assembling crates?

ART. Beer-box dividers.

GADG. At what an hour?

ART. Forty cents. And then / I meet –

GADG. And at this time, you're earning…

ART. Round about two thousand.

GADG. That's, a week.

ART. Yeah, but the point is / that I meet –

GADG. We all thought that was cute.

ART. The point is, that I meet this girl.

GADG. Oho.

ART. Called Rosie.

GADG. The beer-box divider.

ART. No, she was a secretary.

GADG. You and secretaries.

ART. But the point is, nothing happened. I just found her, very...

GADG. Secretarial.

ART. She'd lost her fiancé, in the war...

GADG. You found her attractive.

ART. Not for that reason.

GADG. And you told her?

ART. Hell, no. But I did tell Mary.

GADG. You told Mary.

ART. Yes. And I kept saying, there was nothing, I'm just telling you, I'm being honest, for Christ's sake, you're my wife, I'm telling you about my feelings. And she was furious.

GADG. No shit.

ART. She said that I'd betrayed her.

GADG. Ditto.

ART. But you know what? I don't think it's just about the girl.

GADG. Well, you don't say.

ART. No, really, here's the thing. I don't think Mary can cope with my career. I think she thinks that I'm two-timing her with theatre. My career's competing with my marriage.

GADG. Just your career?

ART. And I sometimes think she wants me as the bookworm from the shtetl and I want the showbiz and America.

GADG. And why not.

ART. And so, since then, since telling her, my home has been a battlefield. Or, like a courtroom. You know, interrogating? Cold?

GADG. I know interrogating.

ART. We hardly talk. Except for kids and schedules.

GADG. I know kids and schedules. And the thing you're thinking in your head.

ART. Like yes, sure, jumping in the Studebaker and heading west.

Pause.

GADG. The delectable 'Miss Bauer'.

ART. Partly.

GADG. Partly?

ART. Largely. But, I / can't –

GADG. So the question is, I guess you have to ask yourself, if you do that, what you want to do, how will it feel? To her, the kids. But, most of all, to you.

ART (*in agony*). I know.

Pause.

GADG. Did she tell you, she's in Cliff's new movie? Above the title? That's if it gets / put out –

ART. That's who, / Miss Bauer?

GADG. Miss Bauer.

ART. How do you know?

GADG. She writes me long and passionate letters. Largely about you.

ART. Largely?

GADG. Exclusively.

ART. So does Molly know, about your, extramarital…

GADG. She knows some.

ART. So how does she find out? You tell her?

GADG. Hell no. Last time, Paula Strasberg ratted on me.

ART. What, Paula from the Group?

GADG. The Method actress, speaking from the heart. She felt her character would feel that my wife ought to know.

ART. And how did Paula know?

GADG. Ah. Observation.

ART. What did she observe?

GADG. There's three classic tells, she says. You should know this.

ART. Go on.

GADG. Looking at each other's wristwatches. Eating off each other's plates. And putting your hand on the other's lower back.

ART. And Paula spots...

GADG. Kid didn't wear a watch.

ART. And so Molly packs you off to...

GADG. Dr Mittleman.

ART. Yeah, me too. Not Dr Mittleman.

GADG. To sort us out.

ART. Make confession of our sins.

GADG. By way of the beguiling thesis that the key to solving problems in the present and the future is the past. And, as the sainted Sophocles reminds us, how it can shudder back to life.

ART. *Eff*ective memory.

GADG. And you want Oedipal? Get this. When Day does decide to leave, she takes the kids back to *my* mother.

ART. But she's not, you're not breaking / up –

GADG. As you observe. But –

ART. But this isn't what you wanted us to talk about.

Pause. He throws the football to GADG.

GADG. I want you to talk about what you want to talk about.

He throws the football back to ART.

ART. Thank you, Dr Lowenstein.

GADG. Your shrink?

ART. Who helpfully insists the crucial thing is being true to what he charges thirty-five bucks an hour to identify as me.

GADG. Yours too?

ART. Whereas – in these times – I tend to think the crucial thing is being true to something else.

GADG. What, your wife?

ART. Well, yes, sure, Mary. But I was thinking of – what we used to call the Cause.

Slight pause. He throws the football back to GADG.

GADG. Combatting the lackeys of imperialism.

ART. That's the one.

GADG. As opposed to psychiatry, it's all the individual's fault.

ART. 'We're all guilty.'

GADG. Oedipus Schmoedipus.

ART. Our dads lost everything because they hadn't processed childhood trauma.

GADG. Hey, but you know what we used to say?

ART. What's that?

GADG. 'Sure the Party's down on Freud, but that doesn't mean…

ART *and* GADG.…you shouldn't love your mother.'

They laugh.

GADG. Whereas it used to be, when our fathers failed, we took revenge by taking up the Cause. But then we found an even better way.

ART. What's that?

GADG. Success. Fame. Riches. Or, as you put it, 'my career'.

He throws the ball to ART, *who catches it and puts it down.*

Cos what I'd pay thirty-five bucks a pop for is someone who believes the worst betrayal's of yourself.

ART. I don't think I've betrayed myself.

GADG. No, but nor have Morris Carnovksy or Joe Bromberg or any of the Group Theatre guys who went out west to make their fortunes.

ART. And who refused to name names and got blacklisted and lost their whole careers.

GADG. The thing you have, now, in such abundance.

Pause.

ART. Yes, I'm sorry. I haven't had to face it.

GADG. There won't be a Broadway Ten.

ART. Not yet.

GADG. Can you see it? The House Committee summons Oscar Hammerstein?

ART. I can't see it now. But then, I couldn't see them summoning Larry Parks.

GADG. I heard Roy Huggins told them that he'd name names but he wouldn't spell them.

ART. But still, they're finks.

GADG. And Jack Warner named Arthur Miller and Elia Kazan.

Pause.

ART. I don't know why.

GADG. You don't?

ART. I never joined.

GADG. You didn't?

ART. Never – quite.

GADG. I just assumed – you used to talk about what people said at meetings.

ART. I went to meetings. Writers' meetings.

GADG. What kind of writers?

ART. Party writers. So they were usually terrible.

GADG. The meetings or the writers?

ART. Both.

GADG. And you signed stuff.

ART. I signed petitions all the time.

GADG. Art, I need to talk about my trip to Hollywood.

ART. What, for the Oscars?

GADG. Not just the Oscars.

ART. Speak.

GADG. I'm afraid for our friendship.

ART. What? Why?

GADG. I'm afraid that if I tell you this, we may not stay friends.

ART. Because you went to the coast?

GADG. Because of who I saw there.

ART. Gadg, I know about Miss Bauer.

GADG. You do.

ART. You saw her on the trip?

GADG. I did.

ART. This trip?

GADG. But as ever, she was…

ART. Passionate about me. Right.

GADG. Your picture's on her bedside table.

ART. How do you know?

GADG. She told me, when I saw her, on the trip.

ART. You 'saw' her.

GADG. Yup.

Slight pause.

ART. Huh.

GADG. You know, it's funny. The Group folks move west, for the movies. She wants to move east, for the stage.

Slight pause.

Look, of course, it didn't mean a darn –

ART. That's what I said to Mary.

GADG. But it didn't. But I think it would for you.

ART. Would what?

GADG. Mean a darn.

Slight pause.

ART. She's a lovely thing. She's never read a play. She's what you always want – an audience who is completely innocent.

GADG. That's what you want – an audience?

ART. Well, if I do, I haven't had it. But you have.

GADG. And I saw some other people.

ART. Keeping busy.

GADG. No. That morning, the day before the Oscars, I was picked up from the airport by a car.

ART. So what?

GADG. And on the seat was a copy of the *Hollywood Reporter*. Clearly there for my attention.

ART. Yuh?

GADG. With the headline: 'Kazan subpoenaed for secret session at the House Un-American Activities Committee.'

ART. You've been subpoenaed? To appear?

GADG. Yeah.

ART. And when is this?

GADG. When was this.

ART. What d'you mean, when was this?

GADG. I mean, it's 'was' not 'is'.

ART. You mean, this has already happened?

GADG. Back in January.

ART. January?

GADG. Yuh. In secret session.

ART. But, the *Hollywood Reporter*...?

GADG. Not so secret.

ART. And you, what, you told them...?

GADG. That I'd been in the Party, for eighteen months, in 1934 to '6.

ART. That's all?

GADG. That's all.

ART. So you didn't name –

GADG. So I didn't name. And that fact, too, was in the *Hollywood Reporter*.

    ART *breathes deeply.*

ART. Well, thank Christ for that.

    Slight pause.

    I thought...

GADG. I know what you thought. And that night I 'saw' Miss Bauer.

ART. Well, as I / say...

GADG. And the next day I had lunch with Darryl Zanuck and some other guys from Fox. And afterwards he told me I should go back to the committee, as they would demand, and give them names.

ART. Well, sure –

GADG. That's if I ever wanted to have lunch in Hollywood again.

ART. But, for/tunately –

GADG. And that evening *American in Paris* won the Oscar.

ART. A disgrace.

GADG. And I came back east, and had lunch with Cliff Odets.

ART. You said, he said –

GADG. And we agreed to name each other.

Pause.

ART. To name each other?

GADG. Yuh.

ART. To the House Committee.

GADG. Yuh.

ART. And that makes it alright? As long as it's just – each other?

GADG. No.

ART. No, it's not alright?

GADG. No, it's not just each other.

Long pause.

In fact, I'm naming Paula.

(*Smiling*.) Not because, she snitched on me.

ART. And – and, she *knows* this?

GADG. Sure she knows.

ART. So it's just Cliff and / Paula?

GADG. No, it's not just Cliff and Paula.

Pause.

It's everyone who was in the Group, who was in the Party. They were the people who I knew, and they are the people I am naming.

Pause.

ART. The Group Theatre.

GADG. It shocks you there were people in the Group who joined the Party?

ART. No, Gadg. That's not what shocks me.

GADG. You know, I feel we're in denial here.

ART. *We're* in denial?

GADG. Sure. About the rain.

ART. You know, I think I'd prefer it if you'd just betrayed / me –

GADG. I think there's an umbrella in the woodshed.

He turns to go out. MISS BAUER *stands there.*

MISS BAUER. Your memory. Of course it wasn't my place. It was the Bel Air, where you were staying for the Oscars. I came at one-thirty a.m., and slipped into the bed beside you, as was my wont, as you were wont to say. And I told you I was going to marry Joe DiMaggio, the baseball star, and we'd never do this again. But not till afterwards.

GADG *turns back to* ART, *as if to say something. But then he goes out.* ART *picks up the ball and throws it into the trees. Then he sits on the log.*

Ahem.

ART *turns to her.*

You're getting wet.

ART. So are you.

MISS BAUER. Don't think so. So you know what he'd do now. If he was your director.

She goes and sits next to ART *and whispers in his ear. He smiles.*

ART. Midsummer. Blisteringly hot. Setting off the hydrant in the street.

Slight pause.

MISS BAUER. And what you're thinking now. That maybe, when I was with Gadg, I'd think of what it might be like with you.

Re-enter GADG *with an umbrella.* ART *squeezes* MISS BAUER's *hand.*

GADG. Umbrella.

GADG *puts the umbrella up.*

ART. In fact, it's stopped.

GADG. Still spitting.

GADG *closes the umbrella and sits by* ART *and* MISS BAUER *on the log.*

ART. So who the hell else are you naming? Tony Kraber? Bromberg?

GADG. Obviously. The Party meetings took place in his dressing room.

ART. Carnovsky?

GADG. You want I name names to you?

ART. I want to know why you're naming names to anyone.

GADG. So wouldn't you inform on Nazis?

ART. Gadg. Paula and Cliff aren't Nazis.

GADG. No, but what they, what we / supported –

ART. On the other hand, there's a guy on the committee who calls Jews 'kikes'.

GADG. Not any more.

ART. And you think he's the only one?

GADG. Look, I don't like the committee. I don't like what
they're doing or how they're doing it. I think it stinks. But
it's happening. And I don't see why I should sacrifice my
career in defence of stuff I don't believe in any more.

ART. So it's the money?

GADG. No, Art, it's not the fucking money. It's doing what
I want to do, and what I'm good at doing. It's directing
movies. It's directing plays, like yours.

ART. And when you say 'stuff'?

GADG. Well, I don't believe the defendants in the Moscow
show trials were guilty.

ART. Show trials.

GADG. I don't think the Nazi-Soviet pact was the greatest blow
for the international proletariat. And I sure as hell don't think
there was a plot by Jewish doctors to kill Stalin. Though
maybe there should / have been –

ART. And labour rights? Opposing the war camp? Race
equality? The New Deal?

GADG. Oh, yeah, sure, I believe in the New Deal. And the
other stuff. Just not all the other stuff. I mean, for Christ's
sake, Art, do you?

ART. Gadg, why did you join?

GADG. Because a lot of all the other stuff was yet to happen.
Or we were yet to know about it. That's, as opposed to now.
When we know, that far from living in a radiant future of
peace and plenty, half the Russian Party ended up in the
labour camps or dead.

ART. I mean, what did it feel like?

GADG. Who's this, Dr Mittelman?

ART (*standing, to go*). I can't do this. I got a four-hour drive.

MISS BAUER (*prompting* GADG). Greenwich Village.

GADG. But that's not the fucking question.

MISS BAUER. Paula Strasberg.

ART. What is the fucking question?

MISS BAUER. Bakery.

GADG. Not why I joined, but why I left.

ART. So tell me why you left.

He sits again.

GADG. You know, sometimes I think I wiped it out...

ART. No shit.

MISS BAUER *whispers in* GADG*'s ear.*

GADG. Okay. So, it was 1936 –

MISS BAUER. *Is* 1936 –

GADG. *Is* 1936, and I'm in Paula Strasberg's apartment in
the Village, at a meeting of the Party cell of the Group /
Theatre –

MISS BAUER *whispers to him.*

Okay, which is above a bakery –

MISS BAUER. Which makes...

GADG....which makes the best chocolate babka in New York.
And it's our cell, from the / Group –

MISS BAUER. And they're baking that night, so the apartment
fills up with the smell of chocolate and cheese...

GADG. – and you can smell the cooking from the bakery, and
we've been summoned to discuss my reservations about the
Party's latest proposal, which was – is – that we demand the
Group be run on collective lines, on the impeccably Leninist
principles of democratic centralism.

MISS BAUER. To which you had responded –

GADG. To which I had responded that this didn't seem an
entirely workable idea.

MISS BAUER. And there's this guy...

GADG. And there's this 'Leading Comrade' from the Party, who accuses me of being 'a lackey of the bosses' if not an out-and-out class traitor. And I realise that I am not being asked to justify my stance, but to confess my manifest iniquities.

MISS BAUER. So you can spurn them...

GADG. So I can spurn them in the future and be welcomed back into the fold. And naturally, being a democratic organisation, the cell was asked to vote on whether they should go with my lickspittle lackeydom or walk the Party line. And Tony, Joe and Paula do the latter, and I'm the only vote for me.

MISS BAUER. So you walk out, your nostrils tingling with the sweet aroma of the night.

GADG. So it's not just the Moscow trials. Or rather, it is, but the Greenwich Village version. So I don't think it's a betrayal of the workers of the world when I decide to stop pretending to be someone else and burn my Party card next day.

Pause. MISS BAUER *stands watching.*

ART. Well, I didn't have a Party card.

MISS BAUER. But, still, what happened to your folks...

ART. But I realised that what had happened to my folks and your folks was terrible and there had to be a better way of doing things, not in Russia in the radiant future, but here and now. And if you don't think that any more, that's fine and dandy. But don't expect me to agree.

He stands, makes to go. But MISS BAUER *blocks him.*

MISS BAUER. And your father couldn't read, and your mom resented it, because she could polish off a novel in an afternoon.

ART *turns back to* GADG.

ART. Hey, did I ever tell you? My mom met this young man in the New York Public Library on 42nd Street and he asked her what she was reading.

MISS BAUER. Cue Milkshake.

ART *sits*.

ART. And they went to have a milkshake in a nearby soda
fountain and she said she'd pay him two bucks a pop to
come round in an afternoon to talk with her about the books
that she was reading.

MISS BAUER *sits between* ART *and* GADG.

MISS BAUER. And she'd lend him books, and sometimes he'd
lend her.

ART. And I'd listen in.

MISS BAUER. And you'd smell the musty odour of the books.

GADG. And this is going where?

MISS BAUER. And then after the crash...

ART. And it was 1933.

MISS BAUER. *Is* 1933. When I was seven. Which is why you
have to hold my hand, and run your thumb up and down my
thumb, and tell me how it felt to have to lend your pop – who
used to have his own chauffeur – a nickel for the subway.

ART. And the guy comes round one last time. Because by now
my mother didn't have two bucks to pay him, and she'd
sold her books, except one that she'd lent him, and he was
bringing back. And afterwards we went out into the street.

MISS BAUER. And you said you couldn't understand how this
could happen, your father with his business and your mom
with all her books.

ART. And he told me that in fact, it was all quite
comprehensible.

MISS BAUER. If you saw it like he saw it.

ART. If you saw it through the prism of the struggle between
capitalists and workers, and the fact that ultimately
the system would break under the weight of its own
contradictions, and it was the workers who would win. And
that through a study of the past, I too could understand the
present and thus change the future.

MISS BAUER. And how did that make you / feel –

ART. And by this I felt I was among the most vital people in the world.

GADG. Yeah, I remember that.

MISS BAUER *whispers to* ART.

ART. And yeah, sure, it was a blistering hot day, and some kids had set off a fire hydrant in the street. And he said, Artie, look at those kids. If it's too hot, if it's unbearable, if they can't take it any more, then they set off the hydrant, and get cool.

MISS BAUER. And it was the last time you saw him.

ART. And it was the last time I saw him. And three years later, I heard he'd gone to Spain to fight the fascists in the civil war. Maybe to die. In fact, to die.

MISS BAUER. Hot darn.

ART. And having those beliefs and sticking to them was what I owed to him and me. And if I betrayed the other people who believed that, Gadg, and who fought for that belief, then who was I actually betraying?

GADG. But you didn't go to Spain.

ART. No. I guess I felt – I had this craving to write plays.

GADG. And, yet, still, the possessor of the Truth of Everything.

MISS BAUER. And thus the most vital person in the world.

ART. And a big-mouth from the Party tells you to confess your sins. Which weren't sins, but opinions you had every right to hold. And you said 'no'.

MISS BAUER. Yes.

GADG. And I'm supposed to sacrifice my career for the sake of people who did exactly that, to me?

ART. And that's a reason?

GADG. Cos you know what? I'm not sure I ever was a communist. Deep down, I was just mimicking, what other

people thought I ought to feel and be. The Kazan Mask,
Marxist-Leninist variety. And I've been lying to myself, for
seventeen years now, and I think it's time I quit.

ART. So who's the me that you've been lying to?

GADG. Well, he doesn't take thirty-five bucks an hour to find.

Slight pause.

He's a success. He's good at what he does. And he won't be
pushed around.

MISS BAUER *takes* GADG*'s hand.*

MISS BAUER. And he loves his wife and kids and likes
his dinner on the table dead on seven with the service
monogrammed just so and screwing pretty girls down alleys
and in the backs of cars.

She takes ART*'s hand.*

And he wishes things could feel the way they were, when he
was listening to the talk about the books, and sniffing at their
musty smell.

GADG. And he won't say he's acting for his reputation. Cos
you know what? I couldn't give a shit about what other
people think of me.

He stands up.

And if we're talking personal, wasn't it your brother stayed
home to look after Mom and Pop while you went off to
college? That's before he joined the army and went off to
fight the Nazis?

MISS BAUER (*to* ART). You fought the Nazis. You're still
fighting them.

ART. Alright. You want it personal. You left the Party because
your friends betrayed you for the sake of what they thought
to be some higher cause. At the time, in fact, the cause of
beating Hitler. And now you're going to betray the people
who betrayed you. Even though of course they all left the
Party too, not so long after.

MISS BAUER. And you gotta know how much –

ART. And I don't think you know quite how much those people love you. The people who you go and whisper to in the corner of the room. But I do know that if you asked them, some time down the line, how did it feel when you first heard that Gadg Kazan had squealed on you? They'd say: 'It felt like Gadg was whispering to me.'

GADG. Fuck you.

MISS BAUER. Zip-a-dee-doo-dah. Cue Rain.

She stands and goes out. Pause. ART *stands.*

ART. So, would you betray me? Would you name my name?

Pause.

Are you going to name me?

GADG. I'm asking you – not to betray me.

ART. What, name *your* name?

GADG (*obvious*). No. No. I mean…

Slight pause.

I'm being honest. I'm telling you about my feelings.

He puts his hand out. It's raining again.

Geez, it's April. Let's go in.

He makes to go.

ART. So are you asking me or telling me?

GADG. I didn't want you to turn on the radio and hear the names.

ART. That isn't what I asked.

Pause.

GADG. I'm asking you. Of course I'm asking you. You're my lousy brother.

He sits down again.

And of course I still believe in the New Deal and labour rights and all that stuff. I just don't go with the methods and kowtowing to the Soviets. I didn't leave the left, Art. It left me.

ART. And have you thought about your kids? How they'll feel, about their father telling tales?

GADG. Kids. Well, that's pretty personal.

ART. And your work? Your pictures? Do you still believe in them?

GADG. Of course I still believe in them.

ART. *Boomerang!*?

GADG. The story of a grave miscarriage of justice.

ART. *Gentleman's Agreement*?

GADG. An attack on good old-fashioned anti-Semitism.

ART. And our work? *All My Sons*? Banned for performance by the US Army?

GADG. Art, *All My Sons* is a great play.

ART. And *Salesman*? Picketed by the Legion? Accused of being commie prop/aganda –

GADG. Art, come on, I still believe in *Salesman*. All your work. Of course I do. In fact, I'd like to hear about the new one.

ART. Would you direct it?

GADG. Would you want me to?

ART. If you wanted to.

GADG. Of course I'd want to.

ART. Whatever it's about?

GADG. Whatever.

Pause.

ART. I can see your point, about not being able to make movies. After all, I could still write in jail.

GADG. You're not going to jail.

ART. Because there's no blacklist on Broadway.

GADG. Exactly.

ART. So you could work there.

GADG. I know. But I guess – I have this craving to make movies.

ART. And the government should not require you to betray your friends in order that you should. You shouldn't have to choose between what's right and what seems best for you. The government should not be in that line of business, here in America.

Pause. GADG *says nothing.*

And, Gadg, this can't last, surely. In the long run. But while it is the way it is, then I guess you have to ask, if you do what you say you want to do, how will you feel?

GADG *looks at* ART.

Because of course you're right. It's not about the other people. Don't worry what I think. The thing you've got to ask yourself is, how it's going to feel to you. The you you want to be.

Pause. There's a moment – are they going to embrace?

Gadg.

GADG. Art.

They embrace. It's awkward and stiff, the arms go in the wrong places. But it happens.

Well, thanks. Shall we go in?

Scene Five

Back in the house. DAY *hands* GADG *a drink. She has one herself.*

DAY. Kids fed. Kitchen cleaned. The pipeman cometh. You?

GADG. Me?

DAY. What did Artie say.

GADG. He thinks that his career is breaking up his marriage.

DAY. About your giving evidence.

GADG. He asked if I was going to name him.

DAY. But he wasn't in the Party.

GADG. So he says.

DAY. And do / you – ?

GADG. And I've no reason to – to disbelieve him.

DAY. I guess, he did that 'peace' conference thing, at the
    Waldorf.

GADG. Yeah.

DAY. And he signed pro-Party statements.

GADG. He'd say, against the prosecutions.

DAY. But surely, it's at least a possibility –

GADG. Well, he attended meetings.

DAY. What kind of meetings?

GADG. Writers. Party writers. He said that they were terrible.

DAY. What, the meetings or the writers?

    GADG *acknowledges the joke.*

    And when you told him? What did he say?

GADG. When I told him?

DAY. You did tell him?

GADG. Sure, I told him. And I said I didn't see why I should
    sacrifice my future for the sake of his past.

DAY. What 'past'? I thought you said / he never –

GADG. Well, the Party writer meetings. The Waldorf. And he
    had this friend who died in Spain.

DAY. Well, you don't say.

GADG. And he said if I named names I'd be doing what the Party did to me.

DAY. Oh, yes?

GADG. Betraying friends.

DAY. I hope you said, that's friends who are doing the same thing.

GADG. Not all of them.

DAY. And I trust you asked him if he'd have informed against the Nazis.

GADG. And he said that Cliff Odets and Paula Strasberg aren't Nazis.

DAY. And that was all he said? That you were going to betray your friends?

GADG. No, he said that this wouldn't last. It wouldn't matter in the long run. And I must do what feels right to me.

Pause.

DAY. So then you won.

GADG. I won?

DAY. The argument.

GADG. Yeah, I guess I did.

DAY. And will he back you?

GADG. I don't know.

DAY. Did you ask him?

GADG. Sure I asked him. He didn't say he wouldn't –

DAY. Not enough. And he said that you should do what you feel is right?

GADG. That was the gist of it.

DAY. He's a writer, Gadg. What exactly did he say?

ART *enters, with a towel. He's dried his hair.*

ART. Great towels.

GADG. Anatolian cotton.

DAY. Gadg should have gotten you an umbrella.

GADG. I did. He spurned it.

ART *folds the towel and puts it down.*

DAY. Do you want a drink?

ART. No thank you.

GADG. As he said. Long drive.

DAY. Then coffee?

ART. Hot tea?

DAY. Gadg.

Pause.

GADG. Hot tea.

He picks up the towel and goes out.

DAY. Good walk?

ART. Well, it was raining.

DAY. How's Mary?

ART. I think you asked that. Fine.

DAY. So everything's just swell with you young folks?

ART. So everything's just swell.

He sits.

DAY. So did you talk about the new play?

ART. In a sense.

DAY. Do you want Gadg to direct it?

ART. Ditto.

DAY *sits.*

DAY. So you talked about what he's going to do.

ART. What he's *going* to do?

DAY. Correct.

Slight pause.

ART. I didn't / think –

DAY. Artie. We don't like the committee. How it goes about its business. But –

ART. Gadg thought it stank.

DAY. But that's not all he thinks.

ART. No, he went on to say he didn't see why he has to defend people who betrayed him.

DAY. For which he'll be pilloried by most everyone you know.

ART. No he won't. Unless he names names.

DAY. And what of your beliefs?

ART. What, you're asking me what I believe?

DAY. I am.

Pause.

ART. Alright, then. I believe what Gadg believed. That capitalism failed America.

DAY. Your family.

ART. Our families. The Depression. Hitler. The World War.

DAY. And Russia as the radiant future of mankind?

ART. That's how it seemed.

DAY. And you still feel that?

ART. I still believe we need to change this country.

DAY. And so you trot off to the Waldorf and you snuggle up to Soviet placemen in the pocket of the MGB, all in the name of 'International Understanding and World Peace'.

Enter GADG with tea for ART.

ART. Look, Day, I'm not a spokesman for the Soviets. I just
stand by my plays. Particularly the ones which Gadg
directed.

DAY. And you think Gadg doesn't do that?

ART. You tell me.

GADG. I told you. I stand by your plays and my films.

He puts the tea down.

ART. As you said.

GADG. Your tea.

DAY. Films which are obviously about how this country's still
the finest in the world.

ART (*to* GADG). Oh, yeah?

DAY. Mainly because when we find we have a problem – which
God knows we do – we admit it and set about to solve it.
And one problem that we have at present is that the secret
agents of a country that cannot and will not admit it has a
problem, that wants to turn this country into that one, have
bored their way into our businesses, our labour unions,
our universities, our entertainment industry and indeed our
government. And stirred up labour disaffection and fanned
the flames of racial discontent. And I'm proud to be married
to a man who rather than contribute to that problem has
decided to be part of the solution.

ART (*to* GADG). And you haven't left the left, it's left you?

Pause.

DAY. And you know, sometimes I wonder, Artie, if you're that
committed to the creation of a workers' paradise, why you
didn't take the red veil, like Gadg did? Why you didn't swim
in the river, but just paddled on the edge? Why you were a
mimic of a Marxist, not the real deal? Maybe it's because
that's what you're best at.

ART. What I'm best at?

DAY. Mimicking.

ART. Molly, I didn't come here to have you / shout at me –

DAY. Cos if you really believed it, Artie, wouldn't you have joined? Or fought in Spain, like your heroic friend? Or gone to Germany, and actually fought fascism? Rather than just attend a few lousy Party writers' meetings?

ART realises what GADG has told DAY. He's still. Then he looks at the Scrabble. A mordant little laugh.

ART. 'Topical.' But I didn't realise quite how much.

Slight pause.

DAY. Queer, isn't it. Informers are the villains. But whistle-blowers are the heroes. What's in a name.

ART (*to* GADG). So if it really was a point of principle, why wait *till* you were subpoenaed? Why not do it anyway?

DAY. Gadg is doing it right now. As you told him to.

ART. As I *told* him?

Pause.

DAY. What did you say?

ART I said a pile of things. As you seem to be aware.

DAY. About what Gadg should do.

ART. I said this wouldn't last forever.

DAY. Or, it wouldn't matter in the long / run.

ART. So the thing he's got to think about is how he'll feel about himself, when this was over.

Pause.

DAY (*to* GADG). 'And I should do what feels right to me.'

Pause.

You think you said the same thing. Jesus.

Slight pause.

You really think you said the same?

ART. But, I see it's all decided.

GADG. Yup. It is.

ART. You know, I wish you were just doing it for the money.

DAY. And you're not concerned with your career?

ART. Not enough to be a stool / pigeon –

DAY. That's the career that's breaking up your marriage?

A moment. Then ART *stands.*

ART. Alright. I think I'm done here.

GADG. Where are you going?

ART. I'm going to my car.

GADG. Where are you going in your fucking car?

ART. To Massachusetts.

DAY. Why?

ART. I'm researching my next play.

GADG. You said you weren't sure it was the next play.

ART. Well, I am now.

DAY. What's in Massachusetts?

ART. Salem.

Pause.

DAY. So what's the play?

ART. You know what the play is.

DAY. Tell us.

Pause.

ART. Why d'you want to know?

GADG. / Because I always want to know –

DAY. / Because it's set in Salem.

Pause. ART *sits.*

I'm guessing, 1600s? People called Abigail and Ezra? Kids dancing naked in the woods?

ART. Alright. If you want this.

DAY. Yes, I want this.

ART. Well, sure, it's set in 1692.

GADG. So, historical.

ART. In a society that has recently been at war. And may soon be again. And which has transferred that sense of threat from outside forces inwards, against its own.

GADG. Sounds familiar.

ART. Sure does.

DAY. Go on.

ART. And this society decides it's threatened by a secret force which challenges the very foundations of its being.

DAY. Don't tell me, let me guess.

ART. A force which can infect your livestock or wither your crops or kill your unborn children.

DAY. And which, no doubt, looks suspiciously akin / to the –

ART. Which recruits the most vulnerable and suggestible. Whose followers take their orders from the very fount of evil.

DAY. Naturally.

ART. Who promises his acolytes a new life in a new land of unimaginable abundance and delight in which all men can enjoy an equal share.

DAY. And his acolytes are I would guess the poor and indigent…

ART. Folks without property who can't defend themselves when they're accused by hysterical young girls of being in league with Satan.

DAY. And then, I'd imagine, the net widens…

ART. Yes, and it catches respected figures in its mesh.
Particularly if their neighbours think they've got above
themselves or are in dispute about the title to a property.

DAY. Or they fancy writing someone else's movie...

ART. And so they too are hauled up and accused of witchcraft.
And if someone 'feels' you're guilty then you are. And so
the only real defence is to confess your sins and to prove the
sincerity of that confession by naming someone else. Well,
preferably more than one. Maybe even ten.

DAY. The Salem Ten. Of course.

ART. And in a year of apocalyptic madness, twenty guiltless
people – guiltless of course because there is no witchcraft –
were put to death.

Slight pause.

And I had this thought, that it might be, if we came to
understand what happened then, we might understand what's
happening in the here and now.

Pause.

DAY. But you're not... You're not saying it's the same.

ART. Well, you know, I think I am.

DAY. But you said it: there weren't any witches.

ART. No.

DAY. But you're not suggesting there aren't communists.

Pause.

ART. It's an analogy.

DAY. It's a false analogy. Because now it's true.

ART. Is it?

DAY. You don't think it's true that the communists control the
electrician's union?

ART. It's not illegal to be a communist.

DAY. Nor is it illegal to expose what they've done and what
they're doing.

ART. No, that seems to be compulsory.

DAY. Artie, the thing you need to ask, is if you understand
    the people of this country any more. The folks who live
    round here, who believe in the committee and its work. Not
    the movie crowd, or the college graduates, or the pointy-
    heads in the fancy papers or the *Review of Books*. Not
    the cosmopolitan elite in New York and DC, who think
    the country should be run by them and for them. But the
    ordinary Joes who live in states you only stop for gas in,
    but who love the place they live in and believe in what
    they think and want their government to protect it. 'We the
    People.' Don't you trust the people to do the right thing, if
    they know the truth?

ART. Hey, but you know what? In truth? I'm being unfair to the
    citizens of Salem. Because at least, at last, one of them had
    the courage to do right. And stand up and say 'no'.

DAY. To witchcraft.

ART. And after him came two, and three, and five, and they
    were joined by priests and judges, and the waves went back.
    And you know, maybe the first guy said what he said because
    he didn't want to be complicit in sending people – maybe
    some of them his friends – to die. Because the guy he wanted
    to be true to was himself. Because he cared about his name.

GADG. So, what are you saying? Not about three hundred years
    ago.

ART. I'm saying that there's someone who could stop this
    madness, Gadg. You of all people. The best director in
    America. Theatre and film. The east coast and the west.
    If you stood up, and said 'no', you could stop it. Now. By
    standing up. By being true to you.

DAY. He doesn't want to stop it.

ART. No? No, really?

    Pause.

GADG. This is the next play. This is the play you want me to
    direct.

ART. This is my next play. I'd love you to direct it. Why
    wouldn't I? But I'd much prefer if you could find it in
    your heart to be that guy. And blow the whistle on what's
    happening in this country.

DAY. Oh, so it's okay to blow whistles if / the people you're –

GADG. Art. All I'm going to do is to turn a light on what
    you call the darkness of the day. On things like Day being
    edged out of a magazine she loved by the agent of a foreign
    government, and secret meetings to dispossess our friends
    of a theatre company that was their life. Yeah, sure, I've left
    the left. I do think that most everything of value I've gained
    in my life – like the chance to do your plays – has been
    about this system – this liberal democratic and yes capitalist
    system – which is why, no, I don't want to change it for
    another system where if you try to blow the whistle on the
    government they send you to a concentration camp. And it's
    worth remembering that without this country, Art, without
    America, your folks would have stayed there in their little
    Polish village and you'd all be dead.

    Pause.

ART. And you don't think democracy is under threat? You don't
    think it needs protecting?

DAY. That's what he's doing.

GADG. And I think you need to ask yourself, what you're
    protecting.

ART. What's that?

GADG. I think that you're protecting what you were.

ART. And you're betraying what you were.

GADG. I was betrayed by what I was.

ART. Cos sometimes, Gadg, I look at all of this, and think, if we
    were wrong, then maybe we were right to be.

DAY. What, right to be wrong? And Gadg is wrong because
    he's right?

ART. I'm saying, what I was is what I am.

GADG. Which is why I'm asking you not to betray me.

Slight pause.

ART. What do you mean?

DAY. He just wants you to stand up for him.

ART. For him?

DAY. For what he's going to do.

ART. I'll defend him from the rooftops if he doesn't do it.

GADG. It's not her decision.

ART. It's what you've both decided. It was never asking me. It was always telling.

GADG. No, it wasn't. I've just made up my mind.

ART. Oh, why?

GADG. Because you're prepared to do to me what you're accusing me of doing to others.

ART. What?

GADG. Betraying friends.

Pause.

Or, in this case, a lousy brother.

Slight pause.

For the sake of – your good name.

Pause. ART *stands.*

ART. I guess that's all I have.

Pause.

Thanks for the drink.

DAY *stands.*

DAY. And so? Are you going to denounce him? Gadg? Are you playing 'get the traitor to the cause'?

ART. I'm not playing anything.

DAY. So what happens when you're asked to sign a letter to the *Times*? Or address a meeting? Would you cross the road to speak to him? Are you going to betray the person who made your career? Is that the person that you want to be?

Pause.

ART. Okay. I won't sign petitions, or write letters to the papers. I won't speak at meetings. I won't call anyone a traitor.

Pause.

GADG. Thank you.

DAY. And the rest?

ART. But my fear is that this thing's not nearly over. We don't know what it's doing to the things we care about, the things you're doing all this for. What your naming names will do to the plays I write and the movies you direct. Whether we can still write about the world, or just ourselves. Which is why I'll never work with you again.

He turns to go.

DAY. I have a question.

ART. Yup?

DAY. Why won't you denounce Gadg as a traitor? If that's what you think?

ART. Well I guess… because I'm a writer. And my job is looking into other people's souls, and finding bits of me.

DAY. Oh, really?

ART. Best to the kids.

He goes out.

GADG. Corny exit speech.

DAY. Oh, you think so?

GADG. With the little puncture.

DAY. What?

GADG. The kids.

DAY. And finding bits of him in other people's souls. You should remember he said that.

Pause.

GADG. It wasn't really a police state in Joe Bromberg's dressing room. Even in Paula Strasberg's apartment. Darn it, we were actors.

DAY. And darn it, Art's a writer

GADG. And it was one helluva bakery.

DAY *takes his hand. The scene is shifting. She is rehearsing him.*

DAY. Mr Kazan. You gave testimony to the committee on January fourteenth.

GADG. Yes.

DAY. That is correct.

GADG. That is correct.

DAY. You spoke fully about your own membership of the Communist Party.

GADG. That is correct.

DAY. However you refused to identify others.

GADG. Yes. That is correct.

DAY. But now you've changed your mind.

GADG. That's right. I want to make a full statement.

DAY. Full and complete.

GADG. I want to tell you everything I know.

DAY. I was wrong before.

GADG. Because I have decided I did wrong before.

DAY. Accordingly...

Pause. She squeezes his hand.

(*Not prompting now, directly to* GADG.) Remember Artie. Just think of what feels right for you.

Scene Six

We hear GADG *give the list of names, which Arthur Miller heard on his car radio as he drove back from Salem a few days later.*

GADG. Lewis Leverett, co-leader of the unit. J. Edward Bromberg, co-leader of the unit, now deceased. Phoebe Brand, who I recruited to the Party. Morris Carnovsky. Tony Kraber, who recruited me. Paula Miller, later Mrs Lee Strasberg, we are still friends, she quit the Party long ago. Clifford Odets. Art Smith. These are the only members of the unit whom I can recall.

DAY *steps forward with* GADG.

DAY. And we will place a statement in the *New York Times*. And he will stay at home two days then he'll do the rounds. His secretary at the Actors Studio will announce she cannot work for him. And Miller cuts him in the street.

GADG. But he doesn't call me traitor.

DAY. Artie's play about the witches will be called *The Crucible*. No one will quite know what the title means. It won't bomb –

GADG. – but it won't do that great either.

DAY. On opening night, Art will raise a glass and say, 'This one's for Gadg.'

GADG. And I'll make *On the Waterfront*.

DAY. Which will be about a rat or fink or snitch or stoolie.

GADG. Whistle-blower.

DAY. But in this case as the hero.

GADG. And I'll tell my critics to go fuck / themselves.

DAY. And you'll win the Oscar.

DAY *goes out as* MISS BAUER *comes in*.

MISS BAUER. Two of the actors in *The Crucible* will be blacklisted.

Enter ART. GADG *goes out.*

And in 1956, three years later, you'll be summoned to appear.

She has a spiral-bound notebook, which she opens.

ART. Right. My name is Arthur Miller and I'm a playwright.

MISS BAUER. Mr Miller, are you a member of the Communist Party?

ART. No, I am not.

MISS BAUER. Have you ever been a member?

ART. No.

She tears a page from the notebook and holds it up.

MISS BAUER. However is it true that you supported a statement asserting that the aforesaid party is a legal party, and if it loses its rights then we lose our rights also?

ART. I don't recall.

MISS BAUER *looks questioningly at* ART.

But I might well have done.

MISS BAUER. Notwithstanding.

She tears another sheet.

This is a letter to the newspaper condemning the work of this committee and calling for its abolition. Did you support the sentiments therein?

ART. It's possible. I don't remember.

MISS BAUER. Your name is on the letter.

ART. Then I did.

MISS BAUER. So you supported this initiative?

ART. I supported many causes.

MISS BAUER. Doubtless because you agreed with it.

ART. Well, maybe.

MISS BAUER *breathes deeply, then:*

MISS BAUER. Moreover, did you write a play you called *The Crucible*?

ART. I did.

MISS BAUER. Which was widely seen as an attack on this committee.

ART. I don't know why. The play was set in 1692.

MISS BAUER. Come on. People saw it as a parallel.

ART. That's up to them.

MISS BAUER. And as such quite clearly an attack on this committee on behalf of those it has harrassed and persecuted over many years.

Pause.

Huh?

ART. I have to... I've been advised to say...

MISS BAUER. While surely staying true to what you think and feel.

ART. But accepting there's some things I thought and felt then which I don't think now.

MISS BAUER. Papa. You know how envious I am of you.

ART. You're *envious*?

MISS BAUER. When you were thinking – doing all those things, I was being shunted round from home to home like a sack of trash.

ART. I know. But you're not the only one who wants a different life.

MISS BAUER. How so?

ART (*taking her arm*). For the last four years, all I've thought of doing is to put my life-so-far behind me. Heading westward. Being true to me.

MISS BAUER *pulls her arm away.*

MISS BAUER. You stood up to the studios.

ART. Sure. And you stood up to them as well.

MISS BAUER. And you opposed segregation in the south. The woman on the bus they tried to make move to the back?

ART. I do. And you made the Mocambo hire Ella Fitzgerald.

MISS BAUER. And aren't we up against the same thing? Typecasting?

ART. Of course we are. It's just, back in the thirties, p'raps we were too easy on the communists.

MISS BAUER. I thought they were about a better world.

ART. Well, I guess there were things they did in Russia that we didn't know about. Or we did, but didn't think they were important.

MISS BAUER (*takes his hands*). But surely, still. You still believe there has to be a better way? Not in Russia in the future, but in the here and now?

ART. And I guess they didn't act, they didn't always act, in the best of faith.

Slight pause.

As if any of us does.

MISS BAUER. You don't act in *good faith*?

ART. Well, no, I didn't mean...

MISS BAUER. To me that's the most important thing of all. 'Faith. Hope. The Cause.'

She embraces him.

Papa.

Pause.

ART. I wish you wouldn't call me that.

MISS BAUER. I didn't have a father. I can pick and choose.

ART. Just as long... as you're not looking for a saviour.

MISS BAUER. Just as long as you're not looking for a saving grace.

Pause.

You know what I'm feeling now. The man I want to be with is the man who tells the truth tomorrow. Or what's the point of anything?

She closes the notebook and makes to go.

ART. Ask me again.

MISS BAUER. Ask what?

ART. The question.

MISS BAUER. What about?

ART. *The Crucible.*

MISS BAUER *finds the note of the question.*

MISS BAUER. Did you write a play called *The Crucible*?

ART. I did.

MISS BAUER. Which people saw as an attack on this committee.

ART. Did they?

MISS BAUER. Come on, Mr Miller. The play is about witch-hunts against innocent people who lose their livelihoods and some their lives. You did not intend to draw a parallel?

Slight pause.

ART. The comparison is inevitable. Sir.

MISS BAUER. Wuh-hoo.

ART *smiles. He thinks the rehearsal is over. But* MISS BAUER *asks another question.*

Now, sir, please, about these meetings with communist writers – terrible the writers or the meetings both ho-ho – which you attended in New York City.

We are in the hearing. DAY *and* GADG *appear, speaking the words of the House Un-American Activities Committee.* MISS BAUER *is watching.*

GADG. What occasioned your presence?

DAY. Who invited you there?

ART. I couldn't tell you. I don't know.

GADG. Can you tell us who was there when you walked into the room?

Pause.

ART. Mr Chairman, I understand the philosophy behind the question and I want you to understand mine. I am not protecting the communists or the Communist Party. I am trying to and I will protect my sense of myself.

MISS BAUER (*under her breath*). So?

ART. So I could not use the name of another person and bring trouble on him. I ask you not to ask me that question.

DAY. Mr Chairman. I respectfully suggest that the witness be ordered and directed to answer the question as to who it was he saw at these meetings.

GADG. You are directed to answer the question, Mr Miller.

Pause.

ART. I have given you my answer.

MISS BAUER. Zip-a-dee-doo-dah.

MISS BAUER *punches the air with her fist.* DAY *and* GADG *continue to speak as members of the committee.*

GADG. Did you know a man by the name of Kazan?

ART. I did.

GADG. What was your relationship with Mr Kazan?

ART. He was the director of two of my plays.

GADG. And was he subsequently exposed as a communist?

ART. I believe so; yes.

GADG. And did you then in 1953 criticise Mr Kazan as an informer?

ART. No.

GADG. After Kazan had been your producer, worked with you on your plays and came down to Washington and testified before a congressional committee, did you criticise him for that position? Did you break with him?

ART. Are you asking if I broke with him? Is that the question?

GADG. The question is, did you attack him because he broke with the Communist Party and testified before a congressional committee?

ART. I have never attacked Kazan. I will stand on that. That is it.

MISS BAUER *is looking at* ART.

MISS BAUER. That's *it*?

DAY *takes the newspaper and reads*.

DAY (*wrily*). Now, your present application for a passport pending in the Department of State is for the purpose of travelling to England, is that correct?

ART. To England, yes.

MISS BAUER. That's *it*?

DAY. What is the objective?

ART. The objective is double. I have a production which is in the talking stage in England of *A View from the Bridge*, and I will be there to be with the woman who will then be my wife.

GADG *and* DAY *look at each other quizzically;* DAY *goes out.* ART *goes to* MISS BAUER. *She tries to look delighted at the news she has just heard.*

MISS BAUER. Well. Passport. England. Wife.

ART. That's good?

MISS BAUER. That's wonderful.

She hugs him.

ART. And I'll be indicted for contempt of congress, tried, and sentenced to a year in jail.

MISS BAUER. And we'll go to England where I'll make a silly film with 'Sir Larry', actually Laurence Olivier and my pregnancy will fail. And you'll write a movie script for me and it'll be the last film I complete. And then, you'll ask Gadg to direct your play.

And in the play Gadg's new girl plays a character which, for everybody on the planet except – (*Re:* ART.) you, is obviously me. Dead me.

She takes her blonde wig off. Her hair is brown. She is the actress who played her, BARBARA LODEN.

Scene Seven

As GADG *speaks, the set of the next scene, a large rehearsal room, appears. On a stage a trestle table, on which is a microphone, and ashtrays; two chairs behind. We are in 1963.*

GADG. This play is all about the past, and guilt, and things repressed, and how it all comes back. I want the rostra and the steps at different levels. I want it to feel jagged and unsettling. And I want the entrance from the back. And not a doorway, or an arch. A void. But at the back of everything is the watchtower of the concentration camp. The thing you can't escape. That's always looming, all the time. And demanding of us, an answer to the question: are any of us, truly innocent?

I want his past to blow back into his life from the blackness of a void.

ART *goes to the table, takes out a script in a leather binder. He sits down and opens the script. He makes the odd note,*

GADG. Hey, Barbara.

BARBARA. Hey. Daddy. Can we talk?

>GADG *and* BARBARA *exit. Enter* DAY. *She goes to* ART, *at the table*.

DAY. Artie. I'm not sure I ever said this.

ART. What?

DAY. Thank you.

ART. What for?

DAY. Keeping your word.

ART (*gesturing round the room*). I said I'd never work with him again.

DAY. And for this too.

ART. I guess the question is – why he took the job.

DAY. Oh, not 'why did you ask him'?

ART. I don't believe in people being blacklisted.

DAY. And you were sentenced to a year in jail for that belief.

ART. Suspended. Overturned.

DAY. Oh, yes.

ART. And he is uniquely qualified.

>DAY *makes to go; then, an afterthought:*

DAY. Hey, you know what I think?

ART. What do you think?

DAY. That the Artie who refused to testify against his friends was the same one who would not denounce my husband.

ART. What.

>GADG *and* BARBARA *have returned.* DAY *kisses* ART, *smiles, and turns to go. She sees* GADG *about to take* BARBARA*'s arm to look at her watch.* GADG *sees her seeing this, and doesn't take* BARBARA*'s arm.* ART *is still thrown by what* DAY *has just said to him.*

DAY (*calls, to* GADG). Gadg, it's five after ten.

> DAY *approaches* GADG *and* BARBARA.

GADG. Molly, meet Miss Barbara Loden.

> *Slight pause.*

> She's playing Maggie.

DAY. You don't say.

> *A moment, then:*

> Well, what a treat.

> *She holds out her hand to* BARBARA.

BARBARA (*shaking* DAY*'s hand*). I'm so pleased to be acquainted.

DAY. Yes, I'll bet.

> *She turns* BARBARA*'s hand, to see the watch.*

> (*To* GADG.) Oh, sorry. Seven after. How time flies.

GADG. Then we had best begin.

> BARBARA *smiles mock-prettily and goes and sits.*

> So whatcha / think?

DAY. Perfect casting.

> *She goes and sits.* GADG *goes to the trestle.*

GADG. So how ya doin', toots?

ART. Just swell.

GADG. So, ya reckon we should get this barndance under way?

ART. Sure thing.

> GADG *and* ART *at the table.* ART *takes out his notecards as* GADG *taps the microphone for silence.* ART *thinks this is his cue, but* GADG *speaks.*

GADG. Okay, ladies and gentlemen. My name's Elia Kazan, and before I ask the author to read his play – as Chekhov read his plays to the actors of the Moscow Arts Theatre –

I have something of my own to say. As some of you know,
this play is partly about political informers, and I have to tell
you there is a political informer in this room, and that it's
me. Did anyone not know that? Well, you do now.

Slight pause. ART *makes to move the microphone to him.*

ART. Well, I should / say that –

' *But* GADG *carries on.*

GADG. So, why this play, and why me of all people to direct it?
The answer is that it's about a fellow who might seem quite
familiar. Whose father comes from far away, and makes it,
and then loses everything. And his son learns that the only
proper business for a man like him was to fight to overthrow
the system and build something new and better in its place.
And he meets a lovely, smart, well-spoken Catholic girl,
who thinks the same as he does, and he forges a career of
promise and distinction, right here in New York City. And
everything's just swell. Fame, Fortune and Success.

Until his past – our past – shudders back to life. And
threatens everything.

And suddenly, these certainties all fall apart. His wife can't
cope with his desire for other women –

A look to and from DAY.

– and his marriage fails. And the girl he falls for's charming,
simple and, yes, innocent... but he thinks the way of loving
people is to lecture them and they let each other down. And a
man so close he might have been his brother, lets him down
by informing on his friends.

Slight pause.

And what does Art do with these people, in this play? It's
what he always does. He looks into their souls, and – like
any writer – sees himself.

A look to ART.

And finds there are no good guys and no bad guys. We're
all Abel, we're all Cain. There is no saving grace. And he

realises that the public issues he was sure about are actually private issues he's not sure about at all. Whether it's political betrayal, or infidelity, or the petty lies our parents tell us, or we tell them, all the way to complicity with the building of the watchtowers and deciding who will live or die. And the choice is not whether to betray but who.

Slight pause.

So, no heroes. No villains. Only victims. As the world is, here, now, in America?

Slight pause. He turns to speak directly to ART.

Isn't that what you think, Art? Isn't that what it's about? That the Art who wouldn't name names is the Art who has forgiven me? Do you forgive me? Do I forgive you?

He pushes the microphone across to ART.

Otherwise, why the fuck ask me to direct your play?

ART *picks up his notecards, looks at them, puts them away.*

ART. Well, sure. It's a play, like all my plays.

Slight pause.

About the gap between what's right and what seems best for you.

ART *opens the script.*

Act One.

Aftermath

Rehearsals for *After the Fall* began on 24th October 1963. Just short of a month later, on 22nd November, President Kennedy was assassinated, and rehearsals were suspended.

Molly Kazan wrote a poem about Kennedy which was published in the *New York Herald Tribune*, to huge acclaim, including a letter of thanks from Robert Kennedy.

Less than three weeks later, on 14th December, Molly suffered a sudden aneurism of the brain and died in hospital a few hours later.

Marilyn Monroe died of an accidental drug overdose on 5th August 1962.

On 23rd January 1964, *After the Fall* opened to indifferent reviews, but the play was a box office success. Miller's later plays dealt with subjects ranging from the Holocaust to the Great Depression, from Soviet dissidents to the making of *The Misfits*, the film he wrote for Marilyn Monroe. Many of these plays were more successful in Britain than in America, and some were premiered here. Miller published an autobiography, *Timebends*, in 1987.

Elia Kazan continued to direct plays and make movies – notably, *The Last Tycoon* – but also wrote five novels and an autobiography.

Barbara and Kazan married in 1967. In addition to her acting career, Loden became a successful director and screenwriter. Her movie *Wanda* won the International Critics Prize at the 1970 Venice Film Festival. She died of breast cancer in 1980.

In January 1999, the Motion Picture Academy announced that they would be awarding Elia Kazan a lifetime achievement award.

A full-page advertisement in *Variety* condemned Kazan for validating the blacklisting of thousands. Members of the Writers' Guild of America advised people attending the ceremony not to stand or applaud Kazan's award. Outside the ceremony, rival demonstrators gathered. Anti-Kazan slogans included 'Don't Whitewash the Blacklist'. A pro-Kazan demonstrator called him a 'moral giant'.

The award was presented by Martin Scorsese and Robert de Niro. Around half the audience applauded and half did not.

Arthur Miller issued a statement, quoting the blacklisted and jailed screenwriter Donald Trumbo, who insisted that there were no heroes or villains of McCarthyism, just victims. His feelings about that dreadful time had not altered, but Kazan's work deserved to be marked. Thus, he supported Kazan's Oscar. But he did not attend the ceremony.

A Nick Hern Book

Here in America first published in Great Britain in 2024 as a paperback original by Nick Hern Books Limited, The Glasshouse, 49a Goldhawk Road, London W12 8QP

Here in America copyright © 2024 Goodwrite Enterprises Ltd

David Edgar has asserted his moral right to be identified as the author of this work

Cover image: Montage from original photo by © Rebecca Need-Menear; additional image Mary Evans Picture Library; design by Annie Rushton

Designed and typeset by Nick Hern Books, London
Printed in the UK by Mimeo Ltd, Huntingdon, Cambridgeshire PE29 6XX

A CIP catalogue record for this book is available from the British Library

ISBN 978 1 83904 369 7

www.nickhernbooks.co.uk/environmental-policy